# THE
# Premiership
# Football
## Miscellany

I would like to dedicate this book to my wife, Janice,
and our two sons, Marc and Paul.

First published in 2008 by Prion
An imprint of the Carlton Publishing Group
20 Mortimer Street
London W1T 3JW

A CIP catalogue record for this book is available from the British Library

ISBN: 978-1-85375-676-4

Editor: Martin Corteel
Project Art Editor: Paul Chattaway
Production: Lisa Cook

Printed in Great Britain

# THE
# Premiership
# Football
## Miscellany

## JOHN WHITE

**WITH A FOREWORD BY**
## SIR ALEX FERGUSON, CBE

# ⟿ FOREWORD BY SIR ALEX FERGUSON ⟿

I feel extremely privileged to have been a manager in the Premier League since its inaugural season in 1992–93 and even more privileged to be still managing in it today. The Premier League is without question the most attractive and toughest football league in the world. This is not to say that France's Ligue 1, Germany's Bundesliga, Italy's Serie A, Holland's Eredivisie, Spain's La Liga or indeed Brazil's Campeonato Série A or Argentina's Primera División are easy to win, they are just not as demanding or intense over the course of their respective seasons. Some will argue why then a Premiership club does not win the UEFA Champions League year in and year out, which is a valid point, but I just feel that our 38-game season, coupled with Carling Cup, FA Cup and international matches, is the ultimate test of a team's strengths and weaknesses.

Few would disagree when I say that history has shown that the best team in the UEFA Champions League does not always collect Europe's most coveted club prize at the end of a season, whereas the fact remains that the best team over the course of the season will always win the equally coveted Premier League title. Indeed, one only has to look at the vast array of international superstars who currently grace our Premiership: players such as Brazil's Gilberto at Arsenal, the Czech Republic's Petr Cech, France's Nicolas Anelka and Germany's Michael Ballack at Chelsea, England's Steven Gerrard and Spain's Fernando Torres at Liverpool, as well as Argentina's Carlos Tevez and Portugal's Cristiano Ronaldo at Manchester United to see that the Premier League is not just the league where some of the world's best managers want to manage, but also the league where many of the world's best footballers want to test their skills week in and week out.

Since its inception in the 1992–93 season the Premier League has over the last 16 seasons attracted many players who are now quite rightly accredited legendary status. Players with outstanding abilities, mercurial skill, magnificent talent and the odd sprinkling of "genius" have entertained millions of fans up and down the country. There are far too many to list in total, but by way of a fond reminder here are just a few: Eric Cantona, Thierry Henry, Juninho, Jurgen Klinsmann, Robbie Fowler, Peter Schmeichel, Alan Shearer and Gianfranco Zola. Every one of these truly gifted footballers have all left their individual mark in one way or another in the annals of Premiership history, while many from the modern era will no doubt join them.

In closing, I hope John's book will help rekindle many of your own fond memories of outstanding achievements by your own team since the Premiership began, but also provide you with the occasional "I forgot about that" as you leaf through the book page-by-page while at the same time being taken on a wonderful journey covering all that is mystical about this truly wonderful league. Naturally, there is the odd near miss or two thrown into the mix, but then that is football – a game of fantastic highs and lows. Happy reading.

**Sir Alex Ferguson, CBE**

## ⚈ ACKNOWLEDGEMENTS ⚈

Before you commence reading this book, I would like to take the opportunity to pay tribute to all those people who helped me finalise my book into the volume you now hold in your hands.

I would like to personally thank a number of very deserving people, both family and friends: Davy Campbell, Bill Clarkson, Addy Dearnaley, John and Martin Dempsey, Frankie Dodds (aka Dodger), Marty Ferguson, Damien Friel (aka Big Dee), Mickey Morrison, Bobby and Ruth McWilliams my father-in-law and mother-in-law, my own mum Rosaleen Doherty White, my brother David and sisters Danielle, Donna and Michelle.

Thanks also to my publishers and in particular Martin Corteel at Carlton Publishing Limited. Martin and I have collaborated on a dozen projects and we have formed a good team. Martin, I fully appreciate all that you have done for me.

And to my wife Janice and our sons Marc and Paul – you know I could not have done this without you.

However, there is one very special person who is no longer with us that I must pay tribute to, my father John McDermot White. My dad was the leading light behind my love of football and still shines his light brightly on me today.

Miss You Dad

John

# ⚜ INTRODUCTION ⚜

What can I possibly say about the greatest football league in the world that Sir Alex Ferguson hasn't already mentioned? I am sure the Boss will not mind me pinching his own famous line after Manchester United beat FC Bayern Munich at Camp Nou on 29 May 1999 to win the UEFA Champions League and with it the unprecedented treble alongside the Premier League crown and FA Cup: "Football, Bloody Hell!" Having watched countless Premiership games since the inaugural season kicked off in 1992–93, I now know just what Sir Alex meant when he uttered that memorable line.

Football is a game of highs and lows, or "two halves" as the legendary Jimmy Greaves once said. One minute you can be cheering your team on to victory only to see the game turn around in the closing minutes and ecstasy turns to agony as late goals scupper your plans of celebrating the evening. I for one know that I have been in a foul mood, felt down or simply put off my food because my own team, Manchester United, did not win, and I know fans of the other 39 clubs that have played in the Premiership up to the end of the 2007–08 season, will recognize this malaise.

The legendary Bill Shankly once quipped: "Some people believe football is a matter of life and death. I'm very disappointed with that attitude. I can assure you it is much, much more important than that." For many fans Shanks' words ring true in that they live for their football and support their team passionately until the day they die.

Football has always played a huge part of my life from the moment I first saw a young George Best glide across our television screen at home in Belfast as he helped Manchester United to victory in the 1968 European Cup final. From that moment on I was hooked on the Belfast Boy and United and covered my room in posters from *Shoot!* magazine and made sure my mum bought Cookstown sausages for tea. Naturally, I had to have a pair of Bestie's Stylo football boots (although admittedly they never made me play like him!) and I even attended a secondary school in Belfast whose primary uniform colours were red, white and black!

I am extremely passionate about my football and am quite privileged to say that this is my 16th published title on the game I love. I hope you enjoy reading my book and that it helps brings back many fond memories you have from watching your own team grace the greatest football league in the world, the Premier League.

**John White**
June 2008

## ✨ FINAL PREMIERSHIP TABLE 1992–93 ✨

| Pos Team | P | W | D | L | F | A | Pts |
|---|---|---|---|---|---|---|---|
| 1. Manchester United (C) | 42 | 24 | 12 | 6 | 67 | 31 | 84 |
| 2. Aston Villa | 42 | 21 | 11 | 10 | 57 | 40 | 74 |
| 3. Norwich City | 42 | 21 | 9 | 12 | 61 | 65 | 72 |
| 4. Blackburn Rovers | 42 | 20 | 11 | 11 | 68 | 46 | 71 |
| 5. Queen's Park Rangers | 42 | 17 | 12 | 13 | 63 | 55 | 63 |
| 6. Liverpool | 42 | 16 | 11 | 15 | 62 | 55 | 59 |
| 7. Sheffield Wednesday | 42 | 15 | 14 | 13 | 55 | 51 | 59 |
| 8. Tottenham Hotspur | 42 | 16 | 11 | 15 | 60 | 66 | 59 |
| 9. Manchester City | 42 | 15 | 12 | 15 | 56 | 51 | 57 |
| 10. Arsenal | 42 | 15 | 11 | 16 | 40 | 38 | 56 |
| 11. Chelsea | 42 | 14 | 14 | 14 | 51 | 54 | 56 |
| 12. Wimbledon | 42 | 14 | 12 | 16 | 56 | 55 | 54 |
| 13. Everton | 42 | 15 | 8 | 19 | 53 | 55 | 53 |
| 14. Sheffield United | 42 | 14 | 10 | 18 | 54 | 53 | 52 |
| 15. Coventry City | 42 | 13 | 13 | 16 | 52 | 57 | 52 |
| 16. Ipswich Town | 42 | 12 | 16 | 14 | 50 | 55 | 52 |
| 17. Leeds United | 42 | 12 | 15 | 15 | 57 | 62 | 51 |
| 18. Southampton | 42 | 13 | 11 | 18 | 54 | 61 | 50 |
| 19. Oldham Athletic | 42 | 13 | 10 | 19 | 63 | 74 | 49 |
| 20. Crystal Palace (R) | 42 | 11 | 16 | 15 | 48 | 61 | 49 |
| 21. Middlesbrough (R) | 42 | 11 | 11 | 20 | 54 | 75 | 44 |
| 22. Nottingham Forest (R) | 42 | 10 | 10 | 22 | 41 | 62 | 40 |

## ✨ BORO JOY ✨

Of the three clubs promoted to the Premier League at the end of the 1997–98 season (Charlton Athletic, Middlesbrough and Nottingham Forest) only Middlesbrough avoided an immediate drop into the First Division. Boro finished a highly respectable ninth. It was their highest league finish for more than 20 years.

## ✨ MARCHING TO A NEW TROT ✨

On 25 October 2007, Bolton Wanderers unveiled their latest signing – new manager Gary Megson, who left Leicester City to take charge of the Trotters following Sammy Lee's sacking. Bolton lay at the foot of the Premiership table with just five points from their opening ten games. "Gary has demonstrated he has the right temperament for a battle, which this season is undoubtedly going to be," said Phil Gartside, the Bolton chairman.

# ❧ FORMATION OF THE FA PREMIER LEAGUE ❧

As the 1987–88 season began, the Football League was planning how to celebrate the centenary of its formation in 1888. Such plans were soon overshadowed, however, by a threat from ten of the leading teams at the time, most notably Arsenal, Liverpool and Manchester United, to break away from their controlling body and form a new elite Super League that would generative lucrative television money for the clubs concerned.

Matters came to a head in 1991 when the Football Association unveiled its new master plan (*"Blueprint for Football"*) in which the idea of a new Super League to comprise the top 18 clubs at the time was mooted. On 14 June 1991, 16 English First Division clubs began the process of severing their ties with the Football League by putting their names to a document of intent to join a new league, to be known as the FA Premier League. Soon afterwards the remaining six First Division clubs jumped ship and all 22 tendered their resignation from the Football League. On 20 February 1992 the FA Premier League, commercially independent of the Football Association and the Football League, was officially formed. The 1991–92 season ended with Leeds United pipping Manchester United to be crowned the last ever champions of the old First Division. The following season, 1992–93, Manchester United won the inaugural FA Premier League (FAPL), their first championship success in 26 years.

# ❧ THE JEWEL IN THE CROWN ❧

During the 1999–2000 season Manchester United withdrew from the FA Cup at the request of the Football Association so that they could participate in the inaugural FIFA World Club Championship. The FA wanted the jewel of English football's crown to play in Brazil in an effort to help bolster England's chances of hosting the 2006 FIFA World Cup finals. It was the first time in the history of the competition that the reiging FA Cup holders chose not to defend the famous trophy, and while United's Premiership opponents were slogging it out on rock-hard pitches up and down England the United players were basking in the sunshine in Rio de Janeiro.

# ❧ DEADLY DOUG DEPARTS ❧

On 19 September 2006, Randy Lerner replaced 82-year-old Doug Ellis as the chairman of Aston Villa.

## ❧ PREMIERSHIP TALK (1) ❧

"When the seagulls follow the trawler, it is because they think sardines will be thrown into the sea."
*Eric Cantona (Manchester United), February 1995*

## ❧ THE UNCAPPED 300 CLUB ❧

Going into the 2007–08 Premier League season Chris Perry of Tottenham Hotspur had made the most Premiership appearances without ever having been capped by his country. Perry had played more than 300 Premier League games for Wimbledon, Tottenham Hotspur and Charlton Athletic (338 in total). Perry is one of four players to have played in excess of 300 Premiership games without receiving international recognition. In second place in the table of non-capped players was Peter Atherton, with 314 games for Coventry City, Sheffield Wednesday and Bradford City, and third was Jason Dodd, with 306 Premiership games for Southampton. Finally, Steve Watson made 303 Premier League appearances for Newcastle United, Aston Villa, Everton and West Bromwich Albion without England ever calling upon his defensive capabilities.

## ❧ THE BATTLE OF THE BUFFET TABLE ❧

On 24 October 2004, Manchester United ended Arsenal's record 49-game unbeaten run in the top flight with a 2–0 win at Old Trafford. After the game a scuffle broke out between players from both teams, which spread to the changing-room area, with slices of pizza and even pea soup being thrown at Sir Alex Ferguson and several of the Manchester United players. This led to the game being dubbed "The Battle of the Buffet" and resulted in an even more intense and bitter rivalry between the two sides. In the return game at Highbury on 1 February 2005, Roy Keane and Patrick Vieira clashed in the tunnel before kick-off, and Mikael Silvestre was sent off during the game for head-butting Freddie Ljungberg. Despite only having ten men, United won 4–2 to complete a unique treble over Arsenal, having already knocked them out of the League Cup earlier in the season.

## ❧ ARSENE HONOURED ❧

In 2002 Arsene Wenger, the manager of Arsenal, was awarded France's highest decoration, the Legion d'Honneur.

## ❧ THE MAGNIFICENT SEVEN ❧

Since the inception of the Premier League in season 1992–93, only
seven teams have played every season of the league's 16-year history
(includes season 2007–08):

❖ Arsenal ❖
❖ Aston Villa ❖
❖ Chelsea ❖
❖ Everton ❖
❖ Liverpool ❖
❖ Manchester United ❖
❖ Tottenham Hotspur ❖

## ❧ BLUES HAT-TRICK ❧

In season 2005–06, which marked Chelsea's 101st campaign, the
Blues won their second successive Premier League title. It was the
third championship success in the club's history.

## ❧ STICKY TOFFEE ESCAPE ❧

On the final day of the 1993-94 season Everton, league champions
seven years earlier, were in danger of being relegated from the
Premiership. Things were going badly for the Toffees when they
trailed Wimbledon 2–0 at half-time at Goodison Park. However,
with top-flight football for the following season under threat,
Everton turned the game, and their fortunes, around in the second
half, scoring three times to win 3–2 and stay up. Swindon Town
were already relegated going into the final day, and the remaining
two relegation places went to Oldham Athletic, who failed to beat
Norwich City (ironically the team the Everton manager Mike
Walker had managed for the first five months of the season), and
Sheffield United, who lost to Chelsea.

## ❧ 129-YEAR-OLD DEFENCE ❧

Lee Dixon (38), Tony Adams (35), Martin Keown (35) and
Ashley Cole (21) were the Arsenal back four that helped the club
achieve the domestic Double in season 2001–02. Behind them in
goal was 38-year-old David Seaman. They leaked just 36 goals
between them in the 38 Premiership games played and were the
second meanest defence behind the Liverpool back four, who only
conceded 30 goals.

## ❧ DAVID BECKHAM, OBE ❧

David Robert Joseph Beckham was born on 2 May 1975 in Leytonstone, London. In 1989 he signed schoolboy forms with Manchester United and became a trainee in July 1991. On 23 September 1992, David made his United debut in a Rumbelows Cup tie at Brighton & Hove Albion. In May 1996, a Beckham-inspired United became the first English club to win the coveted Double twice following their all-conquering 1993–94 season. On the opening day of the 1996–97 season, David scored perhaps the greatest FA Premier League goal of all time. United visited Wimbledon at Selhurst Park and David sensationally chipped Neil Sullivan in the Wimbledon goal from 55 yards.

On 1 September 1996, David made his full England debut in a 3–1 World Cup qualifying game away to Moldova. However, during the 1998 World Cup finals in France, David was sent off against Argentina at St Etienne. England lost in a penalty shoot-out and many fans and journalists blamed him for England's elimination. He became the target of severe criticism and abuse, but Beckham was undaunted and in 1999 he inspired Manchester United to the treble of FA Premier League, FA Cup and UEFA Champions League. When Kevin Keegan resigned as England coach in October 2000, caretaker manager Peter Taylor appointed David the England captain.

Cometh the hour, cometh the man. On 6 October 2001, Beckham almost single-handedly ensured England reached the 2002 World Cup finals. In their final qualifying game, needing only a draw, England were trailing Greece 2–1 at Old Trafford with just seconds remaining. Beckham stepped up to fire home an injury-time equalizer to book England's trip to Japan and Korea. In the 2002 finals Beckham and England gained revenge on Argentina for putting them out of the 1998 World Cup when Beckham scored from the penalty spot to give England a 1–0 win in Sapporo, Japan.

After helping United to an eighth Premier League title in 2002–03, David joined Real Madrid. It was not all plain sailing with *los galaticos*, however, owing to a few niggling injuries and the team playing second fiddle to Barcelona and Valencia for most of his time there. In season 2006–07 David finally won a medal in Spain after helping Real Madrid to La Liga title, only to pack his bags and follow the sun once again, this time signing for the Los Angeles Galaxy.

### Did You Know That?
On 12 November 2005, David captained England for the 50th time, during their 3–2 friendly win over Argentina in Geneva, Switzerland.

## ❧ SKY FALLS IN ON SKY BLUES ❧

In season 2000–01 Coventry City's luck finally ran out when the Sky Blues lost their top-flight status after 34 consecutive years among the big boys. During the 34 years their highest league placing was sixth.

## ❧ CANNIBAL RACIST REMARK ❧

After helping Nottingham Forest to the First Division Championship title in season 1997–98, and a return to the Premiership, Kevin Campbell left Forest and joined Trabzonspor in Turkey. However, he only stayed with the Istanbul-based club for seven months and left them for Everton following a racist incident involving the club's president, Mehmet Ali Yilmaz, who called Campbell a "discoloured cannibal" and also said about the striker: "We bought him as a goal machine, but he appeared to be a washing machine." In March 1999 he signed for Everton on loan and scored nine Premiership goals in eight games for the Toffees, making him the Goodison Park outfit's leading goalscorer in season 1998–99, despite the fact that he had been at the club for less than four weeks. In the summer of 1999 Campbell signed for Everton on a permanent deal worth £3 million.

## ❧ A SAINTLY DEPARTURE ❧

At the end of the 1996–97 season Graeme Souness, the manager of Southampton, quit his position at The Dell after just one season at the helm and was replaced by Dave Jones from Stockport County. Souness had won the Premier League Manager of the Month Award for April 1997.

## ❧ TROUBLE DOWN THE LANE ❧

On 25 October 2007, Tottenham Hotspur sacked their manager Martin Jol prior to their disappointing 2–1 home loss to Getafe in the UEFA Cup. Three days later Spurs replaced Jol with the Seville manager Juande Ramos and brought in former White Hart Lane favourite Gus Poyet from Leeds United to act as first-team coach under Ramos.

A few days after Jol's sacking, Daniel Levy, the Tottenham chairman, admitted the club made mistakes with the departure of Jol. Much to the embarrassment of Spurs, the news that Jol had been fired was leaked before the game and spread to media and fans as the UEFA Cup clash against Getafe went on.

# FA PREMIER LEAGUE CLUBS 1992–2008

| Club | No. of seasons spent in Premier League | No. of different spells in Premier League | Most recent season in Premier League | All seasons in Premier League |
|---|---|---|---|---|
| **Arsenal**[1] | 16 | 1 | 2007–08 | Ever present |
| **Aston Villa**[1] | 16 | 1 | 2007–08 | Ever present |
| Barnsley | 1 | 1 | 1997–98 | 1997–98 |
| **Birmingham City** | 5 | 2 | 2007–08 | 2002–06, 2007–present |
| **Blackburn Rovers**[1] | 14 | 2 | 2007–08 | 1992–99, 2001–present |
| **Bolton Wanderers** | 9 | 3 | 2007–08 | 1995–96, 1997–98 2001–present |
| Bradford City | 2 | 1 | 2000–01 | 1999–2001 |
| Charlton Athletic | 8 | 2 | 2006–07 | 1998–99, 2000–07 |
| **Chelsea**[1] | 16 | 1 | 2007–08 | Ever present |
| Coventry City[1] | 9 | 1 | 2000–01 | 1992–2001 |
| Crystal Palace[1] | 4 | 4 | 2004–05 | 1992–93, 1994–95 1997–98, 2004–05 |
| **Derby County** | 6 | 2 | 2007–08 | 1996–2002, 2007– |
| **Everton**[1] | 16 | 1 | 2007–08 | Ever present |
| **Fulham** | 7 | 1 | 2007–08 | 2001–present |
| Ipswich Town[1] | 5 | 2 | 2001–02 | 1992–95, 2000–02 |
| Leeds United[1] | 12 | 1 | 2003–04 | 1992–2004 |
| Leicester City | 8 | 3 | 2003–04 | 1994–95, 1996–2002 2003–04 |
| **Liverpool**[1] | 16 | 1 | 2007–08 | Ever present |
| **Manchester City**[1] | 10 | 3 | 2007–08 | 1992–96, 2002–present |
| **Manchester Utd**[1] | 16 | 1 | 2007–08 | Ever present |
| **Middlesbrough**[1] | 13 | 3 | 2007–08 | 1992–93, 1995–97 1998–present |
| **Newcastle United** | 15 | 1 | 2007–08 | 1993–present |
| Norwich City[1] | 4 | 2 | 2004–05 | 1992–95, 2004–05 |
| Nottingham Forest[1] | 5 | 3 | 1998–99 | 1992–93, 1994–97 1998–99 |
| Oldham Athletic[1] | 2 | 1 | 1993–94 | 1992–94 |
| **Portsmouth** | 5 | 1 | 2007–08 | 2003–present |
| Queen's Park Rgrs[1] | 4 | 1 | 1995–96 | 1992–96 |
| **Reading** | 2 | 1 | 2007–08 | 2006–present |
| Sheffield United[1] | 3 | 2 | 2006–07 | 1992–94, 2006–07 |
| Sheffield Wed[1] | 8 | 1 | 1999–2000 | 1992–2000 |
| Southampton[1] | 13 | 1 | 2004–05 | 1992–2005 |

| Sunderland | 6 | 3 | 2007–08 | 1996–97, 1999–2003 2005–06, 2007–present |
| Swindon Town | 1 | 1 | 1993–94 | 1993–94 |
| **Tottenham Hotspur**[1] | 16 | 1 | 2007–08 | Ever present |
| Watford | 2 | 2 | 2006–07 | 1999–2000, 2006–07 |
| WBA | 3 | 2 | 2005–06 | 2002–03, 2004–06 |
| **West Ham United** | 13 | 2 | 2007–08 | 1993–2003, 2005–present |
| **Wigan Athletic** | 3 | 1 | 2007–08 | 2005–present |
| Wimbledon[1] | 8 | 1 | 1999–2000 | 1992–2000 |
| Wolverhampton Wdrers... | 1 | 1 | 2003–04 | 2003–04 |

[1] *Teams in the inaugural Premier League season of 1992–93. Teams in bold were 2007–08 Premier League sides.*

## ❧ A CENTURY LATER ❦

Manchester United's 4–1 win over Middlesbrough in the Premier League on 27 October 2007 was the first time in 100 years that United scored four goals in four consecutive games. The previous occasion came during season 1907-08 when United managed to score four goals or more in four consecutive league games on their way to winning the First Division championship for the first time in the club's history.

## ❧ THE SAS ❦

At the end of the 1993–94 season, Norwich City's Chris Sutton left Carrow Road to join Kenny Dalglish's resurgent Blackburn Rovers, Premiership runners-up to Manchester United, for an English club record fee of £5 million. Sutton would line up alongside Alan Shearer for the 1994–95 season, as the Ewood Park club sought to end their 81-year wait for a League title, and the pair were nicknamed the SAS.

## ❧ TWINKLE TOES ❦

When Glenn Hoddle moved to Chelsea at the start of the 1993–94 season he became the first player-manager in Premier League history. The former Spurs, AS Monaco and England player secured the first European football for the Blues in 20 years when they qualified for the European Cup Winners' Cup, despite losing the 1994 FA Cup final to the Double winners, Manchester United.

## ❧ PREMIERSHIP TALK (2) ❧

"But, at the moment, when I step on the pitch, when I have the ball I know it's mine. It's just a feeling."
**_Thierry Henry_** *(Arsenal)*

## ❧ DOZY PLAYER ❧

On 6 February 2008, Portsmouth's chief executive Peter Storrie stated that Benjani Mwaruwari's transfer to Manchester City failed to take place on transfer deadline day (31 January 2008) because the player fell asleep when he was supposed to be catching an airplane to the north-west. As Storrie put it: "In his own inevitable, wonderful way – and we all love Benji so much – he falls asleep at the airport and misses two planes." In the end Benjani was permitted to join Manchester City two days past the deadline.

## ❧ UNITED STOP ARSENAL FA CUP TREBLE ❧

In season 2003–04 Manchester United prevented Arsenal from reaching their third consecutive FA Cup final by defeating the 2002 and 2003 FA Cup winners in the semi-final. United went on to beat Millwall 3–0 in the final at the Millennium Stadium, Cardiff.

## ❧ 100 PLAYERS WHO SHOOK THE KOP ❧

In 2006 Liverpool produced a list entitled "100 Players who Shook the Kop". Over 100,000 fans of the Anfield club selected their personal Top Ten players in order of impact made and the results were collated to establish a Top 100. Five players who played for the club in the Premier League made the Top Ten (and a sixth, Michael Owen, was 14th):

| | | |
|---|---|---|
| 1 | Kenny Dalglish | 1977–91 |
| 2 | **Steven Gerrard** | 1998–present |
| 3 | **Ian Rush** | 1980–7 & 1988–96 |
| 4 | **Robbie Fowler** | 1993–2001 & 2006–07 |
| 5 | **John Barnes** | 1987–97 |
| 6 | Billy Liddell | 1938–1960 |
| 7 | **Jamie Carragher** | 1996–present |
| 8 | Kevin Keegan | 1971–1977 |
| 9 | Graeme Souness | 1978–1984 |
| 10 | Emlyn Hughes | 1967–1979 |

# ❧ MAN UTD PREMIER LEAGUE FANTASY XI ❧

**1**
Peter
*SCHMEICHEL*

**2**
Gary
*NEVILLE*

**6**
Gary
*PALLISTER*

**5**
Rio
*FERDINAND*

**3**
Denis
*IRWIN*

**4**
Roy
*KEANE*
*(capt.)*

**7**
Eric
*CANTONA*

**8**
Paul
*SCHOLES*

**9**
Ruud van
*NISTELROOY*

**10**
Mark
*HUGHES*

**11**
Ryan
*GIGGS*

*Substitutes*
Fabien *BARTHEZ* • Paul *PARKER* • Steve *BRUCE*
David *BECKHAM* • Cristiano *RONALDO* • Wayne *ROONEY*
*Manager*
Sir Alex *FERGUSON* CBE

***Did You Know That?***
Sir Alex Ferguson managed the Scottish national team at the 1986
FIFA World Cup finals.

## ❧ RELEGATED SIDE MAKE UEFA CUP ❧

Despite finishing in 18th place in the Premiership table in season
2001–02, resulting in relegation to Division One, Ipswich Town
still qualified for the 2002–03 UEFA Cup qualifying round as Fair
Play Award winners.

## ❧ UEFA CHAMPIONS LEAGUE 1-2-3 ❧

As well as the 1999–2000 Premiership champions Manchester
United and runners-up Arsenal, third-placed Leeds United also
qualified for the 2000–01 UEFA Champions League. Liverpool
finished fourth in the Premiership and had to settle for a UEFA
Cup berth, while FA Cup winners Chelsea and League Cup winners
Leicester City also gained UEFA Cup slots.

## ❧ FINAL PREMIERSHIP TABLE 1993–94 ❧

| Pos Team | P | W | D | L | F | A | Pts |
|---|---|---|---|---|---|---|---|
| 1. Manchester United (C) | 42 | 27 | 11 | 4 | 80 | 38 | 92 |
| 2. Blackburn Rovers | 42 | 25 | 9 | 8 | 63 | 36 | 84 |
| 3. Newcastle United | 42 | 23 | 8 | 11 | 82 | 41 | 77 |
| 4. Arsenal | 42 | 18 | 17 | 7 | 53 | 28 | 71 |
| 5. Leeds United | 42 | 18 | 16 | 8 | 65 | 39 | 70 |
| 6. Wimbledon | 42 | 18 | 11 | 13 | 56 | 53 | 65 |
| 7. Sheffield Wednesday | 42 | 16 | 16 | 10 | 76 | 54 | 64 |
| 8. Liverpool FC | 42 | 17 | 9 | 16 | 59 | 55 | 60 |
| 9. Queen's Park Rangers | 42 | 16 | 12 | 14 | 62 | 61 | 60 |
| 10. Aston Villa | 42 | 15 | 12 | 15 | 46 | 50 | 57 |
| 11. Coventry City | 42 | 14 | 14 | 14 | 43 | 45 | 56 |
| 12. Norwich City | 42 | 12 | 17 | 13 | 65 | 61 | 53 |
| 13. West Ham United | 42 | 13 | 13 | 16 | 47 | 58 | 52 |
| 14. Chelsea | 42 | 13 | 12 | 17 | 49 | 53 | 51 |
| 15. Tottenham Hotspur | 42 | 11 | 12 | 19 | 54 | 59 | 45 |
| 16. Manchester City | 42 | 9 | 18 | 15 | 38 | 49 | 45 |
| 17. Everton | 42 | 12 | 8 | 22 | 42 | 63 | 44 |
| 18. Southampton | 42 | 12 | 7 | 23 | 49 | 66 | 43 |
| 19. Ipswich Town | 42 | 9 | 16 | 17 | 35 | 58 | 43 |
| 20. Sheffield United (R) | 42 | 8 | 18 | 16 | 42 | 60 | 42 |
| 21. Oldham Athletic (R) | 42 | 9 | 13 | 20 | 42 | 68 | 40 |
| 22. Swindon Town (R) | 42 | 5 | 15 | 22 | 47 | 100 | 30 |

### *Did You Know That?*

In season 1993–94 Tottenham Hotspur finished 15th in the Premiership table with 45 points, five places above the relegated teams. Exactly one year earlier in the inaugural Premiership season Crystal Palace were relegated after accumulating 49 points (Spurs finished in eighth place in 1992–93).

## ❧ CENTURION TROTTERS ❧

At the end of the 1996–97 season, Bolton Wanderers returned to the Premiership in majestic fashion after reaching 98 points and bagging an impressive 100 goals on the way to winning Division One. Barnsley joined the Trotters in English football's top flight thanks to their runners-up position, the first time they had reached such dizzy heights in the club's history. Crystal Palace ended their two-year sabbatical away from the big boys after clinching promotion to the Premiership via the play-offs.

## ❧ BLACK CATS SCREECH THE LOUDEST ❧

Prior to the Premiership games played over the weekend of 27–28 October 2007 a "Decibel Survey" was conducted by the telephone number service 118 118 to measure the noise factor at all 20 Premier League clubs' grounds. When the resulting "Crowd Noise Table" was published, Sunderland were top, the Black Cats' Stadium of Light measuring a deafening 129.2, while Fulham came bottom. Arsenal's Emirates Stadium, nicknamed "The Library", was 12th in the table.

## ❧ CHANGES DOWN BY THE RIVERSIDE ❧

At the end of the 2000–01 season Bryan Robson resigned as the manager of Middlesbrough after having spent seven years in charge of the club. The writing was on the wall for Robson during the season when Boro appointed the former England manager Terry Venables as his assistant. However, Venables also left at the end of the season after helping the club to the relative safe position of 14th in the table. Boro persuaded Sir Alex Ferguson's right-hand man, Steve McClaren, to take charge at The Riverside.

## ❧ SINGING THE BLUES ❧

When Chelsea beat Manchester United at Stamford Bridge on 29 April 2006, the result gave Jose Mourinho's men their second Premiership crown in a row. In the end the Blues retained their title by eight points from the eight-times Premiership champions Manchester United, with Liverpool one point further back in third place.

## ❧ ARSENE OF THE ARSENAL ❧

When Arsenal won the Premier League in season 1997–98, their French manager Arsene Wenger became the first foreign manager to win English football's top division.

## ❧ TOUGH FOR THE TYKES ❧

Season 1997–98 was Barnsley's first campaign in English football's top flight in the club's 102-year history. In spite of their shock defeat of Manchester United in the FA Cup they were out of their depth in the Premiership and hovered around the relegation zone all season long. They ended up making an immediate return to Division One and have not played Premiership football since.

# ♘ THE BOY WONDER ♞

On 19 October 2002, a spectacular last-minute strike from a 16-year-old named Wayne Rooney gave Everton a 2–1 win over Arsenal in the Premiership at Goodison Park. Rooney's goal against the England goalkeeper David Seaman ended the Gunners' impressive 30-game unbeaten run and propelled the kid from Croxteth on to the world stage. Rooney's wonder strike came five days before his 17th birthday and at the time made him the youngest-ever goalscorer in Premier League history. Rooney grew up supporting Everton, and Duncan Ferguson was his childhood hero. On one occasion after scoring a superb goal in the FA Youth Cup for Everton, Rooney lifted up his shirt to reveal a T-shirt underneath which read: "Once a blue, always a blue." However, the Goodison Park club could only hold on to the prodigious talent for two more seasons. After starring for England at the 2004 European Championships in Portugal he joined Manchester United.

## ♘ IN THE BEGINNING ♞

The following 22 teams resigned from the Football League to contest the new Premiership in the inaugural FA Premier League season of 1992–93:

| | |
|---|---|
| ❖ Arsenal ❖ | ❖ Manchester United ❖ |
| ❖ Aston Villa ❖ | ❖ Middlesbrough ❖ |
| ❖ Blackburn Rovers ❖ | ❖ Norwich City ❖ |
| ❖ Chelsea ❖ | ❖ Nottingham Forest ❖ |
| ❖ Coventry City ❖ | ❖ Oldham Athletic ❖ |
| ❖ Crystal Palace ❖ | ❖ Queen's Park Rangers ❖ |
| ❖ Everton ❖ | ❖ Sheffield United ❖ |
| ❖ Ipswich Town ❖ | ❖ Sheffield Wednesday ❖ |
| ❖ Leeds United ❖ | ❖ Southampton ❖ |
| ❖ Liverpool ❖ | ❖ Tottenham Hotspur ❖ |
| ❖ Manchester City ❖ | ❖ Wimbledon ❖ |

## ♘ EUROPEAN TOFFEES ♞

Everton beat Manchester United, Premiership runners-up in 1994–95 to Blackburn Rovers, 1–0 in the 1995 FA Cup final at Wembley. It meant that the Toffees, despite their lowly Premiership finish of 15th place, still managed to qualify for European football the following season, in the European Cup Winners' Cup, thanks to Paul Rideout's goal.

## ᏸ RONNY'S SEXTUPLE DELIGHT ᏸ

In season 2006–07 Manchester United's Cristiano Ronaldo won five individual awards:

❖ PFA Players' Player of the Year ❖
❖ PFA Young Player of the Year ❖
❖ PFA Fans' Player of the Year ❖
❖ Football Writers' Association Footballer of the Year ❖
❖ Barclays Player of the Season ❖

*Did you know that:*

When Ronaldo was also named in the Premier League Team of the Year he completed an unprecedented sextuple of awards.

## ᏸ KEANO SNARLS AT TAME VIEIRA ᏸ

On 1 February 2005, Manchester United ended Arsenal's 33-game unbeaten home run in the Premiership and inflicted a first home defeat on the Gunners since they lost to Leeds United in May 2003. The Red Devils beat the Gunners 4–2 in a highly charged and exhilarating battle between two sides who between them had won 11 of the 12 Premier League crowns (United 8, Arsenal 3). However, the game will always be remembered more for the pre-match tunnel bust-up between the opposing captains, Roy Keane and Patrick Vieira, which required the intervention of match referee Graham Poll to separate the warring pair. In his post-match interview the Arsenal captain denied accusations that he threatened United's Gary Neville in the tunnel before the game. "I didn't threaten anybody," said Vieira. "They are big enough players to handle themselves. I had a talk with Roy Keane and that's it. Gary Neville is a big lad, he can handle himself. They just played better than us and deserved to win." However, after the match the United captain accused Vieira of lighting the blue touch-paper: "Patrick Vieira is six foot four and having a go at Gary Neville. So I said, 'Have a go at me.' If he wants to intimidate our players and thinks that Gary Neville is an easy target, I'm not having it." Vieira, regarded as Arsenal's hard man with a disciplinary record to back it up, did not take up Keane's offer to go out on to the pitch and "settle the matter" between the pair. When interviewed Sir Alex Ferguson said: "Vieira was well wound up for it. I've heard different stories. Patrick Vieira has apparently threatened some of our players and things like that."

# PREMIER GROUNDS

The following stadia have hosted Premier League football (1992–2008):

| | |
|---|---|
| Arsenal | Highbury, Emirates Stadium |
| Aston Villa | Villa Park |
| Barnsley | Oakwell |
| Birmingham City | St Andrews |
| Blackburn Rovers | Ewood Park |
| Bolton Wanderers | Burnden Park, Reebok Stadium |
| Bradford City | Valley Parade |
| Charlton Athletic | The Valley |
| Chelsea | Stamford Bridge |
| Coventry City | Highfield Road |
| Crystal Palace/Wimbledon | Selhurst Park |
| Derby County | Baseball Ground, Pride Park |
| Everton | Goodison Park |
| Fulham | Craven Cottage |
| Ipswich Town | Portman Road |
| Leeds United | Elland Road |
| Leicester City | Filbert Street, Walkers Stadium |
| Liverpool | Anfield |
| Manchester City | Maine Road, City of Manchester Stadium |
| Manchester United | Old Trafford |
| Middlesbrough | Ayresome Park, Riverside Stadium |
| Newcastle United | St James' Park |
| Norwich City | Carrow Road |
| Nottingham Forest | City Ground |
| Oldham Athletic | Boundary Park |
| Portsmouth | Fratton Park |
| Queen's Park Rangers | Loftus Road |
| Reading | Madejski Stadium |
| Sheffield United | Bramall Lane |
| Sheffield Wednesday | Hillsborough |
| Southampton | The Dell, St Mary's |
| Sunderland | Roker Park, Stadium of Light |
| Swindon Town | County Ground |
| Tottenham Hotspur | White Hart Lane |
| Watford | Vicarage Road |
| West Bromwich Albion | The Hawthorns |
| West Ham United | Upton Park |
| Wigan Athletic | JJB Stadium |
| Wolverhampton Wanderers | Molineux |

BOURNEMOUTH                    DEAN COURT

## ⚜ GERRARD TURNS 400 ⚜

On 28 October 20007 Steven Gerrard played his 400th game for Liverpool and scored in their 1–1 Premier League draw against Arsenal at Anfield. However, the Liverpool captain is some distance behind the club's record appearance holder, Ian Callaghan, who played 848 games for the Anfield club over the course of 19 seasons from 1958 to 1978.

## ⚜ THE FOUR CUPATEERS ⚜

At the start of the 2007–08 Premier League season the four most successful international players, with three trophies each, currently playing for a Premiership club during the season were:

Geremi Nijitap......Newcastle United & Cameroon...2 ACN & 1 OGG
Gilberto Silva.........Arsenal & Brazil.................1 WC, 1 CONF & 1 CA
Kasey Keller..........Fulham & USA.................................3 CGC
Lauren...................Portsmouth & Cameroon...................2 ACN, 1 OGG

*WC – FIFA World Cup; ACN – Africa Cup of Nations; CGC – CONCACAF Gold Cup;*
*CONF – Confederations Cup; CA – Copa America; OGG – Olympic Games Gold*

## ⚜ A HAT-TRICK OF DEPARTURES ⚜

At the end of the 1997–98 season Everton narrowly avoided relegation from the Premiership, finishing one place above the drop zone on goal difference. In spite of having helped Everton preserve their status in English football's top flight for the 45th consecutive season, Howard Kendall resigned as manager. It was the third time the former Everton player had vacated the manager's job at Goodison Park. Walter Smith, the manager of Glasgow Rangers, replaced Kendall.

## ⚜ EIGHT FROM 11 FOR RED DEVILS ⚜

The 2002–03 season was the 11th season of the Premier League, and it was won by Manchester United – their eighth Premiership title. In the final two months of the season Manchester United were simply awesome as they managed to overhaul an eight-point advantage held by the defending champions Arsenal at the beginning of March. Arsenal limped out of the title race in the penultimate game of the season, losing at home to relegation-threatened Leeds United. Once again the Premier League was sponsored by Barclaycard.

## ❧ PREMIERSHIP TALK (3) ❧

"I gave an interview to Radio 4 about the vocabulary of English football and how you quickly become familiar with it."
*David Ginola (Aston Villa)*

## ❧ THE ELITE EIGHT ❧

Only eight English sides have never been outside the top two divisions: Arsenal, Chelsea, Everton, Liverpool, Manchester United, Newcastle United, Tottenham Hotspur and West Ham United. Leeds United and Leicester City were members of this exclusive club until they were relegated to League One (the old Third Division) at the end of the 2006–07 and 2007–08 seasons, respectively.

## ❧ FOUR IN A ROW FOR FERGIE ❧

When Manchester United were crowned FA Premier League Champions in 1992–93, it was the fourth successive year in which Alex Ferguson had guided the club to silverware success:

| | |
|---|---|
| 1990 | FA Cup |
| 1991 | European Cup Winners' Cup & European Super Cup |
| 1992 | League Cup |
| 1993 | FA Premier League |

*Did you know that:*
 Not surprisingly Fergie was named the Premier League Manager of the Year for 1992–93.

## ❧ A MYSTERY ILLNESS ❧

Going into the final game of the 2005–06 season Spurs sat fourth in the Premiership table, the last UEFA Champions League qualifying spot, with Arsenal one place below them. All Spurs had to do was achieve a better result away to West Ham United than Arsenal, who were at home to Wigan Athletic. However, the night before the match a number of the Spurs players fell ill. Spurs approached the FA seeking to delay the kick-off, but the FA refused. West Ham United won the game 2–1, while Arsenal beat Wigan 4–1 to secure the last UEFA Champions League qualification slot and Spurs had to settle for a place in the UEFA Cup.

## ❧ TRACTOR BOY CAUSES BIG SURPRISE ❧

At newly promoted Ipswich Town striker Marcus Stewart was the unknown quantity at the start of the 2000–01 season. However, Stewart's 19 Premier League goals helped his side to fifth in the table and he finished runner-up to Chelsea's prolific frontman Jimmy Floyd Hasselbaink in the Premier League goalscoring table.

## ❧ THE TRIO TO BEAT THE DOUBLE WINNERS ❧

During their Double-winning season of 2001–02 Arsenal only suffered three defeats – at the hands of Charlton Athletic, Leeds United and Newcastle United and all, ironically, at home.

## ❧ LIGHTWEIGHT BANTAMS ❧

In November 2000 Bradford City dismissed Chris Hutchings after just six months in charge of the Bantams and 12 Premiership games and replaced him with Jim Jeffries from Hearts. However, Jeffries could not save the Yorkshire club from relegation, and they dropped into Division One after just two seasons in the Premiership, having finished bottom of the table. They have not returned since.

## ❧ KEEGAN QUITS GEORDIES ❧

On 5 January 1997, Kevin Keegan sent shockwaves around Newcastle after deciding it was time he quit his position as manager. Keegan took over at St James' Park in February 1992 when the Geordies lay second from bottom of the old Second Division. However, Super Kev helped save Newcastle United from relegation and the following season (1992–93) the Magpies won the new First Division Championship title and were promoted to the Premier League. In their first season in the Premiership they finished third in the table followed by a sixth-place finish in 1994–95. The following season Keegan steered Newcastle to the brink of the Premier League title, only for his team to fall away towards the end of the season and finish runners-up to Manchester United. When he walked out of St James' Park, Newcastle were well placed in the Premiership, and they ended the season runners-up to Manchester United once again, but Keegan said that he was quitting because he felt he had taken the club as far as he could. Newcastle United moved swiftly and replaced Keegan with Kenny Dalglish, who had guided Blackburn Rovers to Premiership success in 1994–95.

# ❦ ERIC CANTONA ❦

Eric Daniel Pierre Cantona was born in Paris on 24 May 1966. When he was sensationally transferred from Leeds United to Manchester United in November 1992, some Manchester United fans questioned the signing. Over the following five seasons United won four Premier League titles, two FA Cups and two Doubles. Eric almost single-handedly rewrote the history books of Manchester United.

Prior to arriving at Old Trafford, Eric had played for Auxerre, Montpellier, Nantes and Leeds United. Sheffield Wednesday passed up on the opportunity to sign him when he was on trial with them in 1991, but the Owls' loss was Leeds United's gain when Howard Wilkinson teamed him up with Gordon Strachan and the pair helped Leeds win the last ever First Division title in 1991–92. Strangely, it was a telephone call from Wilkinson to Alex Ferguson that led to Eric joining the Red Devils. The Leeds manager wanted to find out whether Denis Irwin was for sale. Ferguson said he was not, then cheekily asked about Eric's availability. Within days the Frenchman joined Manchester United for a bargain fee of £1 million. On 6 December 1992, Eric made his debut as a substitute for Manchester United in a 2–1 home win over Manchester City. The Frenchman's arrival completely transformed United's performances on the pitch with his skill, his composure, his creativity and his goals.

On a number of occasions Eric's fiery temper got him into trouble both on and off the pitch. In December 1991, he was suspended for calling each member of a French disciplinary committee an idiot at a hearing. And, in January 1995, Eric famously exacted his own revenge on a Crystal Palace fan who verbally abused him as he walked off the pitch following a red card at Selhurst Park – Eric's kung fu moment.

However, Eric will always be remembered for his genius on the pitch, his aura of invincibility, his Gallic flair, his grace and composure, his amazing goals and, not least, his famous turned-up collar. United fans affectionately dubbed him "The King". He once said of Manchester United: "I am in love with Manchester United. It is like finding a wife who has given me the perfect marriage." In 1998, the Football League, as part of its centenary season celebrations, included Eric in its list of 100 League Legends, and in 2002 his remarkable achievements in English football were recognized when he was made an inaugural inductee of the English Football Hall of Fame.

*Did you know that:*
Despite his success with United, Eric Cantona did not play international football after France failed to qualify for the 1994 World Cup finals.

## ⚛ BOSS FOR AN AFTERNOON ⚛

Clive Allen took temporary charge of Tottenham Hotspur for their home Premiership game against Blackburn Rovers at White Hart Lane on 27 October 2007 while the newly appointed manager, Juande Ramos, sat in the stands with Daniel Levy, the club's chairman. Spurs lost 2–1, and Allen's tenure was the shortest in Premiership history: it lasted just a single afternoon, as Ramos took over the reins straight after the game ended.

## ⚛ SIR LES' SIX-PACK ⚛

The much-travelled Les Ferdinand scored just one Premier League goal for Bolton Wanderers in the 2004–05 season. However, it proved to be a landmark goal for "Sir Les", making him the first player to score in the Premiership for six different clubs: Queen's Park Rangers, Newcastle United, Tottenham Hotspur, West Ham United, Leicester City and Bolton Wanderers. Two years later, in 2006–07, Andy Cole (Newcastle United, Manchester United, Fulham, Blackburn Rovers, Manchester City and Portsmouth) equalled his achievement. Six other players have scored in the Premiership for five different clubs:

**Nick Barmby** – *Tottenham Hotspur, Middlesbrough, Everton, Liverpool, Leeds United*
**Ashley Ward** – *Norwich City, Derby County, Barnsley, Blackburn Rovers, Bradford City*
**Stan Collymore** – *Nottingham Forest, Liverpool, Aston Villa, Leicester City, Bradford City*
**Benito Carbone** – *Sheffield Wednesday, Aston Villa, Bradford, Middlesbrough, Derby County*
**Mark Hughes** – *Manchester United, Chelsea, Everton, Blackburn Rovers, Southampton*
**Teddy Sheringham** – *Nottingham Forest, Tottenham Hotspur, Manchester United, Portsmouth, West Ham United*

## ⚛ POOR TRAVELLERS ⚛

During the 1999–2000 season Coventry City played 19 Premier League away games without recording a single victory on their travels (W 0, D 7, L 12, For 9, Against 32). Amazingly, the Sky Blues still managed to finish 14th in the Premiership table thanks to 12 home wins and one home draw at Highfield Road.

## ❧ FINAL PREMIERSHIP TABLE 1994–95 ❧

| Pos | Team | P | W | D | L | F | A | Pts |
|---|---|---|---|---|---|---|---|---|
| 1 | Blackburn Rovers (C) | 42 | 27 | 8 | 7 | 80 | 39 | 89 |
| 2 | Manchester United | 42 | 26 | 10 | 6 | 77 | 28 | 88 |
| 3 | Nottingham Forest | 42 | 22 | 11 | 9 | 72 | 43 | 77 |
| 4 | Liverpool | 42 | 21 | 11 | 10 | 65 | 37 | 74 |
| 5 | Leeds United | 42 | 20 | 13 | 9 | 59 | 38 | 73 |
| 6 | Newcastle United | 42 | 20 | 12 | 10 | 67 | 47 | 72 |
| 7 | Tottenham Hotspur | 42 | 16 | 14 | 12 | 66 | 58 | 62 |
| 8 | Queen's Park Rangers | 42 | 17 | 9 | 16 | 61 | 59 | 60 |
| 9 | Wimbledon | 42 | 15 | 11 | 16 | 48 | 65 | 56 |
| 10 | Southampton | 42 | 12 | 18 | 12 | 61 | 63 | 54 |
| 11 | Chelsea | 42 | 13 | 15 | 14 | 50 | 55 | 54 |
| 12 | Arsenal | 42 | 13 | 12 | 17 | 52 | 49 | 51 |
| 13 | Sheffield Wednesday | 42 | 13 | 12 | 17 | 49 | 57 | 51 |
| 14 | West Ham United | 42 | 13 | 11 | 18 | 44 | 48 | 50 |
| 15 | Everton | 42 | 11 | 17 | 14 | 44 | 51 | 50 |
| 16 | Coventry City | 42 | 12 | 14 | 16 | 44 | 62 | 50 |
| 17 | Manchester City | 42 | 12 | 13 | 17 | 53 | 64 | 49 |
| 18 | Aston Villa | 42 | 11 | 15 | 16 | 51 | 56 | 48 |
| 19 | Crystal Palace (R) | 42 | 11 | 12 | 19 | 34 | 49 | 45 |
| 20 | Norwich City (R) | 42 | 10 | 13 | 19 | 37 | 54 | 43 |
| 21 | Leicester City (R) | 42 | 6 | 11 | 25 | 45 | 80 | 29 |
| 22 | Ipswich Town (R) | 42 | 7 | 6 | 29 | 36 | 93 | 27 |

## ❧ TOP FLIGHT RECORDS ❧

Season 2007–08 was Arsenal's 87th consecutive appearance in the top flight of English football (1920–present) while Everton hold the record for spending the most seasons in the top flight, 107 (1888–1930 & 1954–present).

## ❧ FERGIE'S FLEDGELINGS ❧

At the end of 1994–95, three players who had helped Manchester United win the Premiership title in 1992–93 and the Double in 1993–94 all left Old Trafford. Mark Hughes joined Chelsea, Paul Ince moved to Inter Milan and Everton made United's "Flying Russian", Andrei Kanchelskis, their new club record signing at £5 million. Many viewed the influential trio's departure as the start of the Red Devils' demise, but it actually marked the onset of one of the most successful periods in the club's history, the beginning of Fergie's Fledgelings.

## ❧ TREBLE WINNERS ❧

The 1998–99 season will always be remembered for the fact that Manchester United won an unprecedented treble of Premier League, FA Cup and UEFA Champions League. United and Arsenal went head to head all season long with the Gunners beating the Red Devils twice early in the season (3–0 in the Community Shield at Wembley and 3–0 in the Premiership at Highbury). However, when the season ended, United had beaten the 1997–98 Double winners to the Premiership crown by a single point thanks to a dramatic 2–1 win over Tottenham Hotspur at Old Trafford on the final day; had beaten Newcastle United 2–0 in the FA Cup final at Wembley after knocking the Gunners out in a replay in the semi-final in one of the most exciting FA Cup games ever played; and had won the UEFA Champions League in Barcelona's Camp Nou stadium after scoring two goals in injury time to beat Bayern Munich 2–1. Their UEFA Champions League victory came on what would have been Sir Matt Busby's 90th birthday, 26 May 1999.

## ❧ FRENCH BRIGADE BEGINS AT ARSENAL ❧

Six weeks into the 1996–97 season, Arsenal appointed 46-year-old Frenchman Arsene Wenger as their new manager. Wenger had been working in Japan, having previously managed AS Monaco.

## ❧ MAKE IT A DOUBLE DOUBLE ❧

In season 1995–96, Manchester United completed a remarkable second domestic Double, the first club to achieve this. First of all United reined in Newcastle United's 12-point lead in the Premiership, with the crunch fixture of the season coming at St James' Park on 4 March 1996. United went into the game trailing the Geordies by four points, but a goal from the enigmatic Eric Cantona gave the Red Devils a 1–0 win over the Geordies and provided the momentum they needed to win their third Premiership crown in four years, a truly remarkable achievement. And it was the French genius who gave United the double Double when he scored the only goal of the game to beat Liverpool 1–0 at Wembley in the 1996 FA Cup final.

## ❧ RUSH TRANSFER ❧

On 1 June 1996, Ian Rush left Liverpool (for a second time) and joined Leeds United on a free transfer.

## ❧ TAKING THE BULL BY THE HORNS ❧

When Juande Ramos took charge of Tottenham Hotspur in late October 2007, he brought with him to White Hart Lane his tough fitness trainer from Seville, Marcos Alvarez. The 36-year-old Alvarez is a former professional tennis player and the personal fitness trainer to the bullfighter Fran Rivera. Alvarez is renowned as a hard taskmaster on the training pitch, and on one occasion in his early days at Seville several of the players drew a joke picture of Alvarez with paper stuffed in his mouth so he couldn't instruct them to do any more running. However, the Seville players' fitness paid off when they won the UEFA Cup in 2005–06, the UEFA Super Cup in 2005–06, the Copa del Rey (Spanish Cup) and Spanish Super Cup in 2006–07 and the UEFA Cup again in 2006–07.

## ❧ INAUGURAL PFA TEAM OF THE YEAR ❧

The inaugural PFA Team of the Year was selected following the 2002–03 season and was made up as follows:

1. Brad Friedel............................Blackburn Rovers
2. Stephen Carr............................Tottenham Hotspur
3. Ashley Cole............................Arsenal
4. Patrick Vieira............................Arsenal
5. Sol Campbell............................Arsenal
6. William Gallas............................Chelsea
7. Robert Pires............................Arsenal
8. Paul Scholes............................Manchester United
9. Alan Shearer............................Newcastle United
10. Thierry Henry............................Arsenal
11. Kieron Dyer............................Newcastle United

## ❧ A TRIO OF RELEGATED CITIES ❧

When Derby County beat Manchester United 1–0 at Old Trafford on 5 May 2001 the result meant that Coventry City were relegated after 34 years in the top flight. Derby County ended the season in 17th place in the table, just one place above Manchester City, who along with bottom-of-the-table Bradford City also went down into Division One. Many Coventry and Manchester City fans questioned the Rams' victory, claiming that United, already assured of the championship, simply did not try – in order to ensure that local rivals Manchester City went down.

## ❧ YOU'LL NEVER WALK ALONE ❧

The song "You'll Never Walk Alone" was written by Richard Rodgers and Oscar Hammerstein II for their 1945 musical Carousel. The first occasion when the song was sung at a football match was in 1958 at Old Trafford, the home of Manchester United. At the time the New Mills Operatic Society was rehearsing for their performance of Carousel, and they sang the song at a Manchester United home game to honour the 23 people (including eight Manchester United players) who tragically lost their lives in the Munich air disaster on 6 February 1958. At subsequent United home games the fans sang the song, and they continued to do so until 1963 when the Liverpool band Gerry and the Pacemakers recorded it and released it as a single. The United faithful quickly dropped the song from their Old Trafford match-day repertoire. On 4 November 1963, it reached No. 1 in the pop charts and stayed there for four weeks before being ousted by the Beatles' "I Want to Hold Your Hand". The Liverpool fans then adopted it as the club's anthem, and it is traditionally sung before the start and at the end of all their home games at Anfield. Even Elvis Presley recorded the song, but he only just managed to squeeze into the Top 100 with his version in 1968. In July 1998 Jose Carreras, Placido Domingo and Luciano Pavarotti released an operatic version of the song which reached No. 21 in the UK music charts.

## ❧ A CLEAN SWEEP ❧

Only two players have won the Premier League, the FA Cup, the UEFA Cup and the UEFA Champions League:

❖ **Nwankwo Kanu** ❖
1995 UEFA Champions League
– Ajax
1998 UEFA Cup – Inter Milan
2002 FA Cup – Arsenal
2008 FA Cup – Portsmouth
2002 Premier League – Arsenal

❖ **Paulo Ferreira** ❖
2003 UEFA Cup – FC Porto
2004 UEFA Champions League
– FC Porto
2006 Premier League – Chelsea
2007 FA Cup – Chelsea

## ❧ LIVERPOOL EMPLOY A DIGGER ❧

John Barnes' nickname at Liverpool was "Digger" – not to imply that his displays in the heart of midfield were merely workmanlike, but because his initials are "JCB" – John Charles Barnes.

# ARSENAL PREMIER LEAGUE FANTASY XI

1
David
*SEAMAN*

2
Lee
*DIXON*

5
Sol
*CAMPBELL*

6
Tony
*ADAMS*
*(Capt.)*

3
Nigel
*WINTERBURN*

7
Robert
*PIRES*

4
Patrick
*VIEIRA*

8
Dennis
*BERGKAMP*

9
Ian
*WRIGHT*

10
Thierry
*HENRY*

11
Robin
*VAN PERSIE*

*Substitutes*
Jens *LEHMANN* • Ashley *COLE* • Martin *KEOWN* •
Emmanuel *PETIT* • Nicolas *ANELKA*
*Manager*
Arsene *WENGER* OBE

***Did You Know That?***
Of the British clubs, only Liverpool (16) have played in more European finals than Arsenal (7).

# GEORDIES ON THE SLIDE

After Newcastle United had finished runners-up in the Premiership in the previous two campaigns under the leadership of Kevin Keegan, Kenny Dalglish could only guide the Geordies to 13th place in 1997–98, his first full season in charge at St James' Park. The main problem was that Alan Shearer suffered a serious ankle injury prior to the start of the season that ruled him out of action until February 1998. Another was that both Les Ferdinand and David Ginola were sold to Tottenham Hotspur, and their replacements, John Barnes and Ian Rush, failed to make the grade. However, despite a miserable Premiership campaign, the Geordies made it all the way to Wembley for the FA Cup final, their first since 1974, where they lost 2–0 to Arsenal. Despite losing the final, the Geordies still achieved a place in Europe for 1998-99, in the European Cup Winners' Cup, on account of Arsenal's league and cup Double.

## ❧ PREMIERSHIP TALK (4) ❧

"If I'd had a gun, I would've shot him."
*Aston Villa manager **John Gregory** after Dwight Yorke signed for Manchester United in 1998*

## ❧ MEGA BUCKS ❧

During the 2007–08 season, Premiership salaries and bonuses exceeded the £1 billion barrier for the first time in the Premier League's history, helped by the new £1.7 billion television deal for top-flight games coming into effect.

## ❧ ST PATRICK'S DAY LUCK ❧

On 17 March 2007, Paul Robinson of Tottenham Hotspur and England scored a goal against his opposite number from an 83-yard free-kick. The ball bounced over Watford's on-loan goalkeeper Ben Foster in Spurs' 3–1 win at White Hart Lane. In the 15-year history of the FA Premier League it was only the third time a goalkeeper had scored in a game. The other two goals were scored by Aston Villa's Peter Schmeichel, against Everton on 21 October 2001 (Schmeichel also scored in the UEFA Cup for Manchester United), and Brad Friedel, playing for Blackburn Rovers against Charlton Athletic on 21 February 2004. However, Robinson was the only goalkeeper to score for the winning team.

## ❧ CRAZY GANG LOSE RELEGATION FIGHT ❧

Wimbledon manager Egil Olsen, appointed prior to the start of the 1999–2000 season, was sacked two games before it ended, being replaced by coach Terry Burton. Olsen had led the Norwegian national side to successive FIFA World Cup finals tournaments in 1994 and 1998, but failed to impress in the Premiership. On the last day of the 1999–2000 season Wimbledon lay one place above the relegation zone on goal difference. However, a 3–0 defeat to Southampton at The Dell, combined with Bradford City's surprise 1–0 home win over Liverpool, brought the Crazy Gang's 14-year tenure in the top flight to an end. It was a sad end for the team who had enjoyed a fairytale existence in the Premiership, having only been elected to the Football League in 1977, winning promotion to the top Division in 1986 and achieving a shock 1–0 win over Liverpool in the 1988 FA Cup final at Wembley.

## ❧ GALLAS HAT-TRICK ❧

Arsenal drew 2–2 with Manchester United at Emirates Stadium in a top of the table Premiership encounter on 3 November 2007. Gallas turned the ball into his own net to give United a 1–0 lead at the interval before Cesc Fabregas scored his 11th goal of the season to level the game early in the second half. A goal from Cristiano Ronaldo looked set to give the reigning champions all three points before Gallas scored late in the game. It was the French defender's third goal against United and for a third different team (the others having been scored for Olympique Marseille and Chelsea).

## ❧ NOT AN ENGLISHMAN IN SIGHT ❧

In season 2000–01 not one of the top six teams in the Premier League at the end of the season had an English manager:

| | | |
|---|---|---|
| 1. Manchester United | Sir Alex Ferguson | Scottish |
| 2. Arsenal | Arsene Wenger | French |
| 3. Liverpool | Gerard Houllier | French |
| 4. Leeds United | David O'Leary | Irish |
| 5. Ipswich Town | George Burley | Scottish |
| 6. Chelsea | Claudio Ranieri | Italian |

*Did you know that:*

Peter Reid, a former England international, guided Sunderland to seventh place.

## ❧ LOTS OF POMP ❧

In November 2004 Harry Redknapp left his position as Portsmouth manager and was replaced by the club's executive director Velimir Zajec, who only lasted four months before being replaced by Alain Perrin in March 2005. Harry giuded Pompey to FA Cup glory in 2008.

## ❧ IDLE BOAST ❧

After three games of the 2001–02 season an unfamiliar name headed the Premier League table, Bolton Wanderers. The Trotters had won their opening three games to lead the field, and their manager Sam Allardyce made the bold claim that his side could win the club's first ever championship title. When the season ended, Bolton Wanderers lay 16th in the table, two places above the relegation zone.

## ✌ FIRST PREMIER LEAGUE CHAMPIONS ✌

The first-ever FA Premier League championship title in season 1992–93 was won by Manchester United, their first top-flight crown in 26 years (since 1966–67). Aston Villa, managed by Ron Atkinson, finished runners-up ten points adrift of the champions. United, managed by Alex Ferguson, had chased Villa for most of the season, while Norwich City were also in the hunt for the prestige of being crowned the Premier League's inaugural champions. Amazingly, Norwich City, managed by Mike Walker, led the Premiership at Christmas with a negative goals difference and finished the season in a highly respectable third place to guarantee themselves UEFA Cup football the following season. Newly promoted Blackburn Rovers surpassed all expectations by finishing in fourth place. Spearheaded by their new £3.6m acquisition from Southampton, Alan Shearer, they played an entertaining attacking brand of football and gave Norwich City a 7–1 thumping. Nottingham Forest, European Cup winners in 1979 and 1980, had a dismal season and were rooted to the foot of the table for the vast part of the campaign. Even before Forest were relegated their legendary manager, the outspoken yet colourful Brian Clough, took the decision to retire from football after 28 years in various hot seats across England (Hartlepool United 1965–67, Derby County 1967–73, Brighton & Hove Albion 1973–74, Leeds United 1974 & Nottingham Forest 1975–93). Newly promoted Middlesbrough followed Forest and dropped out of the top flight along with Crystal Palace. Oldham produced a dramatic 4–3 win over Southampton at The Dell on the last day of the season to stay up on goal difference ahead of Palace, who would have stayed up and sent Oldham Athletic down if they had won their final league game. Like Clough, Palace manager Steve Coppell tendered his resignation. Clough was replaced by former Forest player Frank Clark, while Palace appointed Alan Smith as Coppell's successor.

## ✌ FIFA REJECT CLUBS' 39TH STEP ✌

On 14 March 2008, FIFA's executive committee unanimously opposed the Premier League's plan to play a 39th game of the season overseas. Two months earlier the Premier League unveiled its plan to host a 39th round of matches spread across five cities across the world from season 2011–12. "This idea to play a 39th round outside the country does not work. Even the former chairman of the FA, Mr Geoff Thompson, said we should oppose it," said Sepp Blatter the president of FIFA.

## ⚜ FROM DEVILS TO SAINTS ⚜

| Club | Nickname |
|------|----------|
| Arsenal | The Gunners |
| Aston Villa | The Villains |
| Barnsley | The Tykes |
| Birmingham City | The Blues |
| Blackburn Rovers | Rovers |
| Bolton Wanderers | The Trotters |
| Bradford City | The Bantams |
| Charlton Athletic | The Addicks |
| Chelsea | The Blues |
| Coventry City | The Sky Blues |
| Crystal Palace | The Eagles |
| Derby County | The Rams |
| Everton | The Toffees |
| Fulham | The Cottagers |
| Ipswich Town | The Tractor Boys |
| Leeds United | United |
| Leicester City | The Foxes |
| Liverpool | The Reds |
| Manchester City | The Blues |
| Manchester United | The Red Devils |
| Middlesbrough | Boro |
| Newcastle United | The Magpies |
| Norwich City | The Canaries |
| Nottingham Forest | The Reds |
| Oldham Athletic | The Latics |
| Portsmouth | Pompey |
| Queen's Park Rangers | The "R's" |
| Reading | The Royals |
| Sheffield United | The Blades |
| Sheffield Wednesday | The Owls |
| Southampton | The Saints |
| Sunderland | The Black Cats |
| Swindon Town | The Robins |
| Tottenham Hotspur | Spurs |
| Watford | The Hornets |
| West Bromwich Albion | The Baggies |
| West Ham United | The Hammers |
| Wigan Athletic | The Latics |
| Wimbledon | The Dons |
| Wolverhampton Wanderers | Wolves |

## ⚔ UNITED WIN LEAGUE TREBLE ⚔

Manchester United won the 2000–01 Premier League Championship title, their third in succession, and it was the dominant Red Devils' seventh Premiership from the nine contested (their 14th title in total). And for the third consecutive year it was Arsenal who ended up in runners-up spot. Sir Alex Ferguson became the first manager in English football history to win three championships in a row, although Huddersfield Town (1923–24, 1924–25 & 1925–26), Arsenal (1931–32, 1932–33 & 1933–34) and Liverpool (1981–82, 1982–83 & 1983–84) all managed three consecutive First Division championship wins in their history.

## ⚔ A RUUD AFFAIR ⚔

Ruud Gullit, Chelsea's player-manager, helped the Blues to FA Cup glory in his first season in charge at Stamford Bridge. Chelsea's 1997 FA Cup win over Middlesbrough at Wembley not only ended the club's 26-year spell without a major trophy, but also made Gullit the first foreign manager to win a major trophy with an English club.

## ⚔ STRIKER SCORES WITH PAGE 3 PIN-UP ⚔

In 1996 the Wimbledon striker Dean Holdsworth was involved in a highly publicized tabloid scandal when it was revealed he was having an extra-marital affair with Linsey Dawn McKenzie, a Page Three model with the *Sun* newspaper.

## ⚔ WE ALL LIVE IN A ROBBIE FOWLER HOUSE ⚔

Robbie Fowler is reputedly the wealthiest sportsman in Britain. A racehorse owner and property tycoon besides being a footballer, he has a fortune estimated at £28 million. Robbie's property portfolio is believed to contain in the region of 100 properties in and around the Liverpool area. Liverpool fans often playfully teased him at Premiership games by singing, to the tune of "Yellow Submarine", "We all live in a Robbie Fowler house".

## ⚔ TINY TOES ⚔

Jose Dominguez of Tottenham Hotspur (1997–2000) is the smallest player ever to play in the Premier League, he stood only 5 feet 2 inches high.

## ❧ FINAL PREMIERSHIP TABLE 1995–96 ❧

| Pos | Team | P | W | D | L | F | A | Pts |
|---|---|---|---|---|---|---|---|---|
| 1. | Manchester United (C) | 38 | 25 | 7 | 6 | 73 | 35 | 82 |
| 2. | Newcastle United | 38 | 24 | 6 | 8 | 66 | 37 | 78 |
| 3. | Liverpool | 38 | 20 | 11 | 7 | 70 | 34 | 71 |
| 4. | Aston Villa | 38 | 18 | 9 | 11 | 52 | 35 | 63 |
| 5. | Arsenal | 38 | 17 | 12 | 9 | 49 | 32 | 63 |
| 6. | Everton | 38 | 17 | 10 | 11 | 64 | 44 | 61 |
| 7. | Blackburn Rovers | 38 | 18 | 7 | 13 | 61 | 47 | 61 |
| 8. | Tottenham Hotspur | 38 | 16 | 13 | 9 | 50 | 38 | 61 |
| 9. | Nottingham Forest | 38 | 15 | 13 | 10 | 50 | 54 | 58 |
| 10. | West Ham United | 38 | 14 | 9 | 15 | 43 | 52 | 51 |
| 11. | Chelsea | 38 | 12 | 14 | 12 | 46 | 44 | 50 |
| 12. | Middlesbrough | 38 | 11 | 10 | 17 | 35 | 50 | 43 |
| 13. | Leeds United | 38 | 12 | 7 | 19 | 40 | 57 | 43 |
| 14. | Wimbledon | 38 | 10 | 11 | 17 | 55 | 70 | 41 |
| 15. | Sheffield Wednesday | 38 | 10 | 10 | 18 | 48 | 61 | 40 |
| 16. | Coventry City | 38 | 8 | 14 | 16 | 42 | 60 | 38 |
| 17. | Southampton | 38 | 9 | 11 | 18 | 34 | 52 | 38 |
| 18. | Manchester City (R) | 38 | 9 | 11 | 18 | 33 | 58 | 38 |
| 19. | Queen's Park Rangers (R) | 38 | 9 | 6 | 23 | 38 | 57 | 33 |
| 20. | Bolton Wanderers (R) | 38 | 8 | 5 | 25 | 39 | 71 | 29 |

## ❧ GUNNERS UNLUCKY 13 ❧

Arsenal's 2–2 home draw with Manchester United on 3 November 2007 was the first game the Gunners had failed to win in London in season 2007–08 in 13 games played – ten in the Premier League (three away), two in the UEFA Champions League and one in the Carling Cup.

## ❧ TRIPLE HAT-TRICK KINGS ❧

Only three players have scored a hat-trick in the Premier League for three different clubs:

**Kevin Campbell** – *Arsenal, Nottingham Forest, Everton*
**Les Ferdinand** – *Queen's Park Rangers, Newcastle United, Tottenham Hotspur*
**Teddy Sheringham** – *Tottenham Hotspur, Manchester United, Portsmouth*

## ✂ PREMIERSHIP TALK (5) ✂

"Please don't call me arrogant because what I'm saying is true. I'm European champion, so I'm not one of the bottle. I think I'm a special one... We have top players and, sorry if I'm arrogant, we have a top manager."
*Chelsea manager Jose Mourinho, 2004*

## ✂ UNITED'S ALL-TIME TOP TEN ✂

On 19 February 2001, Manchester United's official club magazine celebrated the publication of its 100th edition by publishing an all-time Top 100 of Manchester United players based on a fans' poll conducted by the magazine. Eric Cantona was the fans' No. 1 choice, with the legendary George Best in second place. In addition to United's talismanic French maestro, Cantona, five other players who played for United in the Premier League featured in the Top Ten (indicated in the table with an *). When George Best was asked for his comments on the fans' vote in an interview with the magazine he said: "This side has done the Treble, which many people said would never be done. I mean, winning the Double was considered almost impossible at one time – and they did that twice. But it's a bit unfair to compare eras."

### Manchester United All-time Top Ten Players

1: Eric Cantona*
2: George Best
3: Ryan Giggs*
4: Bobby Charlton
5: Peter Schmeichel*
6: Bryan Robson*
7: Roy Keane*
8: David Beckham*
9: Duncan Edwards
10: Denis Law

## ✂ COVENTRY TOP DOGS ✂

Coventry City were the first ever leaders of the FA Premier League as the 1992–93 season got under way. Their striker Mick Quinn scored 10 Premier League goals in their first six Premiership games.

## ✂ BANTAMS PUNCH ABOVE THEIR WEIGHT ✂

In season 1999–2000 Sunderland's Kevin Phillips scored 30 Premier League goals, making him the Premiership's top goalscorer for the season. His goals helped the newly promoted Black Cats finish in a highly respectable seventh place in the Premiership table.

## ✻ UNITED IN A CLASS OF THEIR OWN ✻

Going into the 2007–08 season only one Premiership club had scored in excess of 1,000 Premier League goals since the inaugural Premiership season began in 1992–93. Not surprisingly, that club was the nine-times Premiership champions Manchester United with a remarkable 1,136 goals from 5,821 matches or 1.95 goals per game.

## ✻ JINXED PLAYERS ✻

Since the inaugural Premier League season began in 1992–93, three players have been relegated with four different Premiership clubs:

**Ashley Ward** – *Norwich City 1995, Barnsley 1998,*
*Blackburn Rovers 1999, Bradford City 2001*
**Nathan Blake** – *Sheffield United 1994,*
*Bolton Wanderers 1996 & 1998, Blackburn Rovers 1999,*
*Wolverhampton Wanderers 2004*
**Nigel Quashie** – *Queen's Park Rangers 1996, Nottingham Forest*
*1999, Southampton 2005, West Bromwich Albion 2006*

## ✻ BRILLIANT BECKS ✻

Manchester United's 22-year-old midfielder David Beckham won the 1996–97 PFA Young Player of the Year Award and a second Premiership winners' medal, his superb form having helped the Red Devils retain the title.

## ✻ A CORRUPT GAME ✻

In September 2006, the BBC aired a *Panorama* programme alleging widespread corruption in the English game.

## ✻ A PAIR OF RUUD AWARDS ✻

Ruud van Nistelrooy won the Barclaycard Player of the Year Award for 2002–03 after helping Manchester United win their eighth Premiership title. The Dutch international also picked up the coveted Barclaycard Golden Boot Award after firing in 25 goals in his 38 Premiership games (equalling his own record of eight goals in eight successive Premiership games), and a massive 44 in all competitions for the champions.

## ❧ THE ENVY OF MILLIONS ❧

Upon taking up his post as manager of Manchester City at the start of the 1995–96 season, Alan Ball said that his job was "the envy of millions". However, the Blues failed to record a win in their opening 12 Premiership games, and a 2–2 draw at Maine Road on the final day of the season saw them relegated. City ended the campaign on 38 points, the same number as Coventry City and Southampton, but Manchester City went down because they had the worst goal difference of the trio. Sadly Alan died in 2007.

## ❧ BLUES BRING REDS DOWN TO EARTH ❧

Manchester United lost their first Premiership home game in over two years on 2 November 1996, losing 2–1 to Chelsea at Old Trafford.

## ❧ FAIR PLAY CITY ❧

Although Manchester City finished the 2002–03 season down in ninth place, three places below the automatic UEFA Cup qualifying slots, they qualified for the UEFA Cup for season 2003–04 – their first season in Europe in a quarter of a century – via the "fair play ranking".

## ❧ ARSENAL'S THIRD DOUBLE ❧

In season 2001–02 Arsenal, runners-up to Manchester United in the three previous Premiership campaigns, finally got the better of the men from Old Trafford. Arsenal, United and Liverpool were involved in a season-long battle for the title, but it was the Gunners' end-of-season form that ensured the Premier League trophy would be sitting in the Highbury boardroom for the first time in four years. The Gunners won their last 13 Premiership games and clinched the title at Old Trafford on 8 May 2002 thanks to Sylvain Wiltord's strike in a 1–0 win over the reigning champions. Arsenal were crowned champions for the 12th time in their history, winning their second Premiership crown and finishing seven points ahead of Liverpool and ten ahead of United. Arsenal then beat Chelsea 2–0 in the 2002 FA Cup final at the Millennium Stadium, Cardiff, to secure their third domestic Double, equalling a feat previously achieved only by Manchester United. Arsenal's Double-winning seasons were 1970–71, 1997–98 and 2001–02, whereas United won all of their Doubles during the 1990s (1993–94, 1995–96 & 1998–99).

# ❧ SIR ALEX FERGUSON CBE ❧

Sir Alex Ferguson has won more trophies than any other manager in the history of English football and has been in charge of Manchester United for more than 1,000 matches. He is currently the second longest reigning manager in Manchester United history with more than 21 years under his belt. The man Reds fans simply call "The Boss" has transformed the Old Trafford club into one of the biggest, richest and most feared clubs in the world. A master motivator of his players, he is also a genius at mind games with other managers, as Kevin Keegan, Arsene Wenger and Jose Mourinho among others will all attest.

Things were nearly very different on two occasions. First, in 1989–90, there were rumblings that United had to win something that season or Ferguson might be shown the door. Lee Martin's 1990 FA Cup Final replay goal was enough to bring silverware to Old Trafford. Then Sir Alex announced his intention to resign at the end of the 2002 season, but changed his mind. The rest is history.

United's domination of the Premier League is phenomenal. Ten titles in the first 16 years and a worst finish of third has set a standard it is hard to see ever being matched. This record does not include cup successes, domestic and European, which has seen United celebrate success in all of them bar the UEFA Cup. United won the inaugural Premiership championship in May 1993, the Reds' first title for 26 years. It lifted an albatross not only from the neck of the club, but also from its manager.

The greatest night of Ferguson's United career came 1999, when United scored twice in the final seconds to snatch the UEFA Champions League from Bayern Munich in Barcelona. United thus completed a unique treble of Championship, FA Cup and Champions League, to go with League and FA Cup doubles achieved in 1994 and 1996.

Alex Ferguson received a knighthood for services to football following the 1999 Champions League success, but his hunger did not subside and, in 2001, he became the first manager to win three consecutive league championships in England. In the Champions League, United had to wait another nine years for another final appearance and, in the Luzhniki Stadium, Moscow, on 21 May 2008, United won their third Champions League crown, defeating Chelsea in the first-ever all-English European Cup final, this coming just ten days after they had achieved their tenth Premiership title, with Chelsea finishing runners-up once again.

*Did You Know That?*
Sir Alex is the only modern manager to have won the league title in both Scotland (Aberdeen) and England (Manchester United).

## ❧ ALL OVER FOR OLE ❧

On 28 August 2007, just 17 days after the 2007–08 Premiership season kicked off, injury forced Manchester United's Ole Gunnar Solskjaer to retire from football. Solskjaer joined United from his local club in Norway, Molde, in 1996 for a bargain £1.5 million. He went on to etch his name in the Old Trafford history books, most famously scoring United's winning goal in the 1999 Champions League final. During his 11 years at Old Trafford the ever-popular Norwegian international won six Premier League championship winners' medals and two FA Cup winners' medals plus the UEFA Champions League. He made 366 appearances for the Red Devils and found the back of the net 126 times, including a goal on his debut as a substitute against Blackburn Rovers.

## ❧ MERRY-GO-ROUND AT THE BRIDGE ❧

In January 1993, Chelsea sacked their manager Ian Porterfield and brought in 1970s Chelsea legend David Webb from Southend United in his place. At the end of the season Webb was not invited to stay on at Stamford Bridge and Glenn Hoddle was appointed the Blues' new manager. Hoddle had been the manager of Swindon Town in season 1992–93 and had guided the Robins to promotion to the Premiership via a 4–3 Division One play-off victory over Leicester City. It was the first time Swindon had reached English football's top division.

## ❧ END OF AN ERA AT HIGHBURY ❧

The 2005–06 season was Arsenal's final season at Arsenal Stadium, Highbury. And the Gunners gave the old stadium a rousing send-off, winning their final game there 4–1 against Wigan Athletic. Thierry Henry scored a hat-trick in the game and kissed the grass at the final whistle. In the summer of 2006 the Gunners moved a short distance to their new 60,000-capacity, all-seater Emirates Stadium.

## ❧ PSYCHO CAN'T SAVE FOREST ❧

Following the departure of Frank Clark on 19 December 1996, Nottingham Forest appointed 34-year-old defender Stuart Pearce as their player-manager on a temporary basis. However, the former England defender, nicknamed "Psycho", could not save Forest from the drop. They finished the season in bottom position. Pearce resigned as manager in March and was replaced by Dave Bassett.

## ❧ PREMIER STADIUMS IN 2007–08 ❧

| Team | Stadium | Capacity |
|---|---|---|
| Manchester United | Old Trafford | 76,212 |
| Arsenal | Emirates Stadium | 60,432 |
| Newcastle United | St James' Park | 52,387 |
| Sunderland | Stadium of Light | 48,707 |
| Manchester City | Eastlands | 47,726 |
| Liverpool | Anfield | 45,522 |
| Aston Villa | Villa Park | 42,573 |
| Chelsea | Stamford Bridge | 42,055 |
| Everton | Goodison Park | 40,569 |
| Tottenham Hotspur | White Hart Lane | 36,240 |
| West Ham United | Upton Park | 35,146 |
| Middlesbrough | Riverside Stadium | 35,049 |
| Derby County | Pride Park | 33,597 |
| Blackburn Rovers | Ewood Park | 31,367 |
| Birmingham City | St Andrews | 30,009 |
| Bolton Wanderers | Reebok Stadium | 28,723 |
| Wigan Athletic | JJB Stadium | 25,138 |
| Fulham | Craven Cottage | 24,600 |
| Reading | Madejski Stadium | 24,161 |
| Portsmouth | Fratton Park | 20,288 |

## ❧ VILLA'S FALL FROM GRACE ❧

Just eight months after their manager Ron Atkinson guided Aston Villa to League Cup success, Villa sacked Big Ron on 10 November 1974 and replaced him with former Villa star Brian Little. Little just managed to keep Villa in the Premiership – they finished one place above the four relegated sides – but it was a huge fall from grace for the team that had finished runners-up to Manchester United in the title race only two seasons earlier.

## ❧ HOUDINI ACT FAILS ❧

Having narrowly avoided relegation form the Premier League at the end of the 1992–93 season on goal difference, Oldham Athletic suffered relegation 12 months later to end their three-year stint in the top flight. Whereas most clubs would have sacked their manager, the Latics continued to place their faith in Joe Royle, who at the time was the longest-serving manager in any of the four English divisions (having served at Oldham for 12 years).

## ✌ TWO OUTTA THREE AIN'T BAD ✌

Aston Villa beat Manchester United 3–1 in the 1994 League Cup final at Wembley to deny the Red Devils a unique Treble of Premier League championship, FA Cup and League Cup. Villa's League Cup triumph earned them a UEFA Cup place for the 1994–95 season although they only finished tenth in the Premiership, and it was a sweet victory for their manager Ron Atkinson, who had been sacked by Manchester United in November 1986 to make way for Alex Ferguson. It was also the second time one of Atkinson's teams denied Fergie the League Cup, during his reign at Sheffield Wednesday he masterminded a 1–0 victory over United in the 1991 final at Wembley.

## ✌ GONGS FOR FRENCH DUO ✌

In the 2003 Queen's Birthday Honours List the Arsenal manager, Arsene Wenger, and the Liverpool manager, Gerard Houllier, were awarded honorary OBEs for their services to British football.

## ✌ WHEN 22 BECAME 20 ✌

The 1994–95 Premiership season was the last season in which the league comprised 22 teams. Prior to the start of the campaign the Football Association had decided to reduce the Premier League to 20 teams for season 1995–96. Consequently this meant that the traditional three-up, three-down system was replaced – for one season only – with a two-up, four-down format. Ipswich Town finished the 1994–95 season rooted to the bottom of the Premiership, having achieved seven wins, while Leicester City finished second from bottom (six wins), Norwich City finished third from bottom (ten wins) and the fourth relegation place went to Crystal Palace (11 wins).

## ✌ WHO ATE ALL THE PIES? ✌

In February 2008, Tottenham Hotspur manager Juande Ramos was asked how he transformed Spurs' season since his appointment in October 2007. Ramos said that the team he inherited from Martin Jol was seriously overweight and had many bad eating habits. According to Ramos, the Tottenham Hotspur squad was 100 kilograms overweight when he and his backroom team arrived at White Hart Lane. However, along with the man he employed as his fitness coach at Seville, Marcos Alvarez, the pair managed to turn fat into muscle with the results bearing testimony to their dietary success.

# ❧ ASTON VILLA PREMIER LEAGUE FANTASY XI ❧

1
Mark
*BOSNICH*

2
J.
*LLOYD-SAMUEL*

6
Ugo
*EHIOGU*

5
Olof
*MELLBERG*

3
Steve
*STAUNTON*

7
Nolberto
*SOLANO*

4
Gareth
*BARRY*
*(capt.)*

8
Lee
*HENDRIE*

9
Darius
*VASSELL*

10
Dwight
*YORKE*

11
Gabriel
*AGBONLAHOR*

*Substitutes*
Nigel *SPINK* • Gareth *SOUTHGATE* • Dean *SAUNDERS*
Ray *HOUGHTON* • Andy *TOWNSEND* • Kevin *RICHARDSON*
*Manager*
Martin *O'NEILL*

### *Did You Know That?*
Aston Villa's most successful manager is George Ramsay. He collected six
league championships and six Fa Cups between 1884 andd 1926.

## ❧ OWEN WINS BALLON D'OR ❧

In 2001 Michael Owen became the first Liverpool player to win
the coveted European Player of the Year award. Commonly referred
to as the "Ballon d'Or" (Golden Ball), it was established in 1956
by *France Football*, a French football magazine, and is awarded
to the footballer deemed to have been the best overall player in
European football during the year. At first only European nationals
playing in Europe qualified, but since 1995 all footballers playing
in Europe have been eligible for the award, regardless of their
birthplace. The winner is chosen by a vote of European football
journalists, one from each of UEFA's member nations. Voters select
their top-five players in order of preference, and points are assigned
to each player, descending from five points for a first-place vote to
one for a fifth-place vote.

## ✂ PREMIERSHIP TALK (6) ✂

"When he said that about Leeds ... I would love it if we beat them. Love it."
*Newcastle United manager **Kevin Keegan**'s rant at Alex Ferguson on Sky Sports, April 1996*

## ✂ TOP GUN HENRY ✂

During the 2005–06 season Arsenal's Thierry Henry scored 27 Premiership goals to end the season as the league's top goalscorer. Amazingly, Henry scored one more goal than the entire Sunderland team managed in the Premiership over their 38 games.

## ✂ FROM RAGS TO RICHES ✂

Blackburn Rovers won the 1994–95 Premier League to claim their first championship success since 1913–14. The team bankrolled by Jack Walker's millions and managed by Kenny Dalglish clinched the title on the final day of the season – ironically at Liverpool, the club where Dalglish enjoyed success both as a player and manager. Despite losing 2–1 to Liverpool they still managed to win the title, as Manchester United failed to win at West Ham United, managing only a 1–1 draw. Jack Walker had taken over as chairman of Blackburn Rovers in 1991, when they were struggling in Division Two and dreaming of past glories. Rovers had not played in the top flight of English football since 1966, the year England won the World Cup, when they finished bottom of the First Division. Indeed, they had not won a major trophy since 1928, when they collected the FA Cup, but Jack Walker's money changed the course of their history.

## ✂ THE REEBOK STADIUM ✂

In the 1997–98 season, Bolton Wanderers welcomed Premiership football to their new 27,000-capacity, all-seater Reebok Stadium.

## ✂ RAFA APPOINTED ✂

On 16 June 2004, Rafael Benitez, the former coach of Valencia, replaced the sacked Gerard Houllier as the manager of Liverpool. Many Liverpool fans were left stunned with the board's decision to get rid of the man who won four cup competitions, including three in one season, during his six-year term as the boss at Anfield.

## ◊ FINAL PREMIERSHIP TABLE 1996–97 ◊

| Pos Team | P | W | D | L | F | A | Pts |
|---|---|---|---|---|---|---|---|
| 1. Manchester United (C) | 38 | 21 | 12 | 5 | 76 | 44 | 75 |
| 2. Newcastle United | 38 | 19 | 11 | 8 | 73 | 40 | 68 |
| 3. Arsenal | 38 | 19 | 11 | 8 | 62 | 32 | 68 |
| 4. Liverpool | 38 | 19 | 11 | 8 | 62 | 37 | 68 |
| 5. Aston Villa | 38 | 17 | 10 | 11 | 47 | 34 | 61 |
| 6. Chelsea | 38 | 16 | 11 | 11 | 58 | 55 | 59 |
| 7. Sheffield Wednesday | 38 | 14 | 15 | 9 | 50 | 51 | 57 |
| 8. Wimbledon | 38 | 15 | 11 | 12 | 49 | 46 | 56 |
| 9. Leicester City | 38 | 12 | 11 | 15 | 46 | 54 | 47 |
| 10. Tottenham Hotspur | 38 | 13 | 7 | 18 | 44 | 51 | 46 |
| 11. Leeds United | 38 | 11 | 13 | 14 | 28 | 38 | 46 |
| 12. Derby County | 38 | 11 | 13 | 14 | 45 | 58 | 46 |
| 13. Blackburn Rovers | 38 | 9 | 15 | 14 | 42 | 43 | 42 |
| 14. West Ham United | 38 | 10 | 12 | 16 | 39 | 48 | 42 |
| 15. Everton | 38 | 10 | 12 | 16 | 44 | 57 | 42 |
| 16. Southampton | 38 | 10 | 11 | 17 | 50 | 56 | 41 |
| 17. Coventry City | 38 | 9 | 14 | 15 | 38 | 54 | 41 |
| 18. Sunderland (R) | 38 | 10 | 10 | 18 | 35 | 53 | 40 |
| 19. Middlesbrough (R) | 38 | 10 | 12 | 16 | 51 | 60 | 39* |
| 20. Nottingham Forest (R) | 38 | 6 | 16 | 16 | 31 | 59 | 34 |

* *Middlesbrough had three points deducted for failing to fulfil a fixture.*

## ◊ A UNIQUE SET OF DOUBLES ◊

Ian Wright (Crystal Palace & Arsenal 1991–92) and Teddy Sheringham (Nottingham Forest & Tottenham Hotspur 1992–93) are the only players to have won the Golden Boot award for finishing as top goalscorer in English foorball's top flight (First Division or Premier League) in a season during which they changed clubs. Following Wright's 29 league goals in the First Division in season 1991–92 (four for Palace and 25 for Arsenal) Sheringham scored 22 Premier League goals in season 1992–93 (one for Forest and 21 for Spurs).

## ◊ TRACTOR BOYS RUN OUT OF GROUND ◊

Just one season after winning the Premier League Manager of the Year Award for guiding Ipswich Town to fifth place in the 2000–01 Premier League, George Burley saw his Tractor Boys relegated to Division One. Ipswich finished 18th in the 2001–02 Premiership table, four points behind Sunderland.

## ✇ 900% INCREASE ✇

On the opening day of the inaugural Premiership campaign in 1992–93 a total of 11 foreign-born players represented the 22 clubs. On the opening day of the 2007–08 Premier League season the figure had risen to 112 players from 20 clubs.

## ✇ UNITED'S DOUBLE YEAR ✇

In 1994, Manchester United retained the Premier League title, the first sponsored by Carling, and also won the FA Cup, beating Chelsea 4–0 at Wembley Stadium in the 1994 final to win the coveted Double. United became only the sixth club to achieve the Double of league championship and FA Cup following Preston North End (1889), Aston Villa (1897), Tottenham Hotspur (1961), Arsenal (1971) and Liverpool (1986).

## ✇ UNLUCKY SEVEN FOR BORO ✇

Arsenal recorded the biggest Premier League win of the 2005–06 season, a 7–0 thumping of Middlesbrough on 14 January 2006. The Gunners goalscorers on the day were Thierry Henry (with three) and Phillippe Senderos, Robert Pires, Gilberto Silva and Alexander Hleb with one each.

## ✇ HOUDINI ACT ✇

Southampton found themselves in the relegation zone all through the 1998–99 season – until April, when they hit a good run of form that ultimately helped them finish 17th in the Premiership table, one place away from dropping into Division One.

## ✇ POMPEY GO UP ✇

The three teams promoted from the First Division to the Premier League at the end of the 2002–03 season were Portsmouth (First Division champions), Leicester City (runners-up) and Wolverhampton Wanderers (play-off winners).

## ✇ PREMIERSHIP TALK (7) ✇

"There is no pressure at the top. The pressure's being second or third."
*Chelsea manager **Jose Mourinho***

## ☙ SUPERMAN PULLS HIS SHORTS DOWN ☙

When Manchester City's Stephen Ireland scored a rocket of a volley in the 67th minute to give his side a 1–0 Premiership home win over Sunderland on 5 November 2007 he celebrated by pulling down his shorts. He had a pair of Superman pants on beneath his shorts. However, his antics would undoubtedly be looked at by the FA. The 21-year-old Ireland had already courted controversy back in September when he admitted lying about the reason for his withdrawal from the Republic of Ireland squad to face the Czech Republic, claiming his grandmother had died. It was later discovered that, much to Ireland's embarrassment, both of his grandmothers were still very much alive … and none too pleased with the antics of their grandson.

## ☙ TROTTERS BREAK PIGGY BANK ☙

At the start of the 1997–98 season newly promoted Bolton Wanderers paid a club record £3.5 million for Wimbledon striker Dean Holdsworth. However, Holdsworth could not prevent the Trotters dropping straight back into Division One, although their fate was not decided until the final day of the season, when they went down on goal difference.

## ☙ ERIC'S BUDDY ☙

In December 1995, Manchester United had a serious injury crisis resulting in the team being bereft of experienced defenders. Alex Ferguson signed William Prunier, a friend of Eric Cantona, who had won a cap for France in 1992, on loan from Bordeaux. Prunier made his debut for United in their 2–1 home win over Queen's Park Rangers on 30 December 1995, but played just one more time for the Old Trafford side, two days later in a 4–1 defeat away to Tottenham Hotspur on New Year's Day 1996, before packing his bags to go back to France.

## ☙ COTTAGERS ALMOST LEFT RED-FACED ☙

In the 2005–06 season Fulham looked in danger of becoming only the third club in the 14-year history of the Premier League to go through an entire Premiership campaign without recording an away win. However, a 2–1 win over Manchester City at Eastlands on the penultimate weekend spared their blushes.

# ◈ CHELSEA PREMIER LEAGUE FANTASY XI ◈

```
                        1
                      Petr
                      CECH


      2          6          5          3
    Albert      John      Marcel     Graham
   FERRER      TERRY    DESAILLY   LE SAUX
              (capt.)


      4               7                8
    Claude          Frank           Arjen
  MAKELELE    LAMPARD Jnr.        ROBBEN


      9              10               11
    Didier      Jimmy Floyd      Gianfranco
   DROGBA    HASSELBAINK          ZOLA
```

*Substitutes*
Carlo *CUDICINI* • Paulo *FERREIRA* • Ricardo *CARVALHO* •
Michael *ESSIEN* • Joe *COLE* • Tor Andre *FLO*
*Manager*
Jose *MOURINHO*

### *Did You Know That?*
Jose Mourinho was linked with the vacant England manager's job in
December 2007, but later denied any interest in the post.

## ◈ THE ELITE FA CUP WINNERS' CLUB ◈

When Chelsea won the FA Cup final in 2007, Ashley Cole became
only the fifth modern player to win four FA Cup winners' medals:

**Mark Hughes:** 1985, 1990, 1994 (Manchester United), 1997 (Chelsea)
**Roy Keane:** 1994, 1996, 1999, 2004 (Manchester United)
**David Seaman:** 1993, 1998, 2002, 2003 (Arsenal)
**Ryan Giggs:** 1994, 1996, 1999, 2004 (Manchester United)
**Ashley Cole:** 2002, 2003, 2005 (Arsenal), 2007 (Chelsea)

In the 19th century, three players, Arthur Kinnaird (The Wanderers
and Old Etonians), Charles Wollaston (The Wanderers) and Jimmy
Forrest (Blackburn Rovers) all won the FA Cup on five separate
occasions.

## ❧ BLACK CATS GO TOP ❧

Sunderland, Coca-Cola Championship winners in season 2006–07, kicked off the 2007–08 Premier League season with a lunchtime fixture against Tottenham Hotspur at the Stadium of Light on 11 August 2007. Sunderland's Michael Chopra's 94th-minute goal put his team, managed by former Manchester United hero Roy Keane, top of the table. Although they did not remain at such dizzy heights for long, finishing the season in 15th place.

## ❧ I'M OFF! ❧

Swindon Town, managed by Glenn Hoddle, won promotion to the Premier League at the end of the 1992–93 season, but Hoddle did not manage the Robins in their first-ever season in the top flight, opting instead to take up an offer to become the player-manager of Chelsea. Chelsea finished 14th under Hoddle, but secured a place in the European Cup Winners' Cup for season 1994–95. The Blues may have lost the FA Cup final 4–0 to a rampant Manchester United, but because the Reds had already claimed the Premier League title, Chelsea took their place in the European Cup Winners' Cup. As for Swindon Town, John Gorman assumed control after Hoddle's departure, but they were relegated after finishing bottom of the table. They have never returned to the Premiership.

## ❧ HEART SCARE ❧

During the 2001–02 season Liverpool manager Gerard Houllier underwent emergency heart surgery after complaining about chest pains during the match against Leeds United at Anfield. The Liverpool manager was advised to rest, and assistant manager Phil Thompson took temporary charge of the Anfield outfit. However, the former Liverpool captain's spell in control of the club resulted in controversy when he sold Kop idol Robbie Fowler to Leeds United for £11 million.

## ❧ KEEGAN OFFERS TO QUIT ❧

Prior to the start of the 1996–97 season Kevin Keegan offered his resignation as Newcastle United manager. The Magpies had been hot favourites to win the 1995–96 Premier League title, only to be overhauled by Manchester United. The board persuaded Super Kev to stay, but five months later, in January 1997, Keegan quit.

# ❦ HARROD'S OWNER SHOPS FOR PLAYERS ❦

After Fulham's promotion to the Premier League at the end of the 2000–01 season the club's flamboyant chairman Mohammed Al Fayed, owner of the famous Harrod's store in London, boasted that his team could win the Premiership crown. The 2001–02 season was the Cottagers' first campaign in the top flight for 33 years, but in spite of the signings of Steve Marlet and Edwin van der Sar they could finish no higher than 13th in the table. Speculation also mounted that Al Fayed was about to swoop for the England captain and Manchester United midfielder David Beckham, but not even his money could prise Becks away from Old Trafford. Al Fayed's side finished 43 points adrift of champions Arsenal.

# ❦ THIRD PLACE RECORD ❦

In season 2007–08, Arsenal finished third in the Premiership behind Manchester United and Chelsea. The Gunners accumulated 83 points from their 38 Premiership games, a record total for a team finishing third, one more than Liverpool's total in 2005–06.

# ❦ A GAME EVERY WEEK ❦

Selhurst Park hosted a Premiership game every week during the 1993–94 season. Wimbledon rented the ground for their Premiership home games while Crystal Palace, the ground's owners, played their First Division home games there.

# ❦ END OF BIG SAM'S TOON HONEYMOON ❦

On 8 January 2008, Newcastle United and their manager Sam Allardyce parted company "by mutual agreement" after he had spent just eight months in the job. Big Sam had been in charge for only 24 games, but had a dismal record of eight wins, six draws and ten defeats, leaving the club 11th in the Premiership table. He became the sixth manager to leave the Geordies in ten years:

| | |
|---|---|
| 1997–98 | Kenny Dalglish – sacked |
| 1998–99 | Ruud Gullit – sacked |
| 1999–2004 | Sir Bobby Robson – sacked |
| 2004–06 | Graeme Souness – sacked |
| 2006–07 | Glenn Roeder – left by mutual consent |
| 2007–08 | Sam Allardyce – sacked |

## ❧ KEEPING THE SHIRT ON HIS BACK ❧

On 10 November 2007, Newcastle United's new billionaire owner Mike Ashley decided to watch the 138th Tyne-Wear derby with the Geordie fans behind the goal at Sunderland's Stadium of Light rather than cause offence by wearing his Newcastle United shirt in the Sunderland directors' box. Ashley had been advised by Sunderland that if he wore his jersey it would be regarded as a provocative gesture. The match ended in a 1–1 draw.

## ❧ UNITED'S 2006–07 TROPHY SWEEP ❧

In a season during which Manchester United claimed their ninth FA Premier League title, a number of other awards also went to the Old Trafford outfit. Cristiano Ronaldo enjoyed the best season of his life, winning the sextuple of PFA Players' Player of the Year, PFA Young Player of the Year, PFA Fans' Player of the Year, Barclays Premiership Player of the Season, Football Writers' Association Player of the Year and a place in the FA Premier League Team of the Year (eight of the 11 selected were United players). Ryan Giggs was presented with the Barclays Premiership Merit Award in recognition of his record of nine Premier League titles, while the man who guided United to their nine Premiership crowns, Sir Alex Ferguson, was named Barclays Manager of the Season.

## ❧ GRASSHOPPER REFUSED WORK PERMIT ❧

In 1997, Christian Gross replaced Gerry Francis as the manager of Tottenham Hotspur. Gross left his job as coach of Grasshoppers Zurich in Switzerland to take up his appointment at White Hart Lane and attempted to bring with him to London his right-hand man at Grasshoppers, fitness coach Fritz Schmid. However, Schmid was refused a work permit by the British authorities and therefore had to remain in Zurich. When, eleven months later, Gross was sacked and replaced by George Graham, he returned to Switzerland to take charge of FC Basel, and by the end of the 2006–07 season he had guided the team to three Swiss championships and three Swiss Cups.

## ❧ SKY BLUES FALL IN ON REDS ❧

On 19 December 1992 Liverpool travelled to Highfield Road and were soundly beaten 5–1 by Coventry City. It remains the Reds' record defeat in the Premier League to date.

## ❧ TOTTENHAM GO DUTCH ❧

In September 2003, Tottenham Hotspur sacked Glenn Hoddle and replaced him in the managerial hot seat with the club's director of football, David Pleat. Pleat took over as temporary manager until the end of the season when a permanent appointment was given to Jacques Santini, formerly the French national coach. Santini's tenure at White Hart Lane only lasted for five months, however, before he was replaced with Spurs' assistant first-team coach, Martin Jol.

## ❧ WALKERS STADIUM ❧

In November 2000, Leicester City announced that the club would move to a brand-new all-seater stadium, the Walkers Stadium, with capacity for 32,000 spectators at the beginning of the 2003–04 season. The new stadium was built next to Leicester City's old Filbert Street ground, and as it turned out the club were able to move into their new home a year early in time for the start of the 2002–03 season.

## ❧ THE RETURN OF THE MESSIAH ❧

Shortly after Christain Gross succeeded Gerry Francis as the manager of Tottenham Hotspur in November 1997, his first move was to appease the continuing hostility towards the club's chairman, Alan Sugar, by bringing back a former White Hart Lane hero, Jurgen Klinsmann. At the end of the 1997–98 season, in which Spurs finished 14th in the Premiership and Klinsmann netted nine times in 15 appearances, the German striker announced that he would hang up his boots after the World Cup finals in France. Klinsmann enjoyed a highly successful playing carer before going on to coach the German national team (2004–06). He won the UEFA Cup twice (in 1991 with Inter Milan and in 1996 with Bayern Munich), won the Bundesliga with Bayern Munich in 1997, was voted German Footballer of the Year twice (1988 & 1994) and English Footballer of the Year in 1995. As a player with the German national team he won the 1990 World Cup and the 1996 European Championships in addition to a bronze medal at the 1988 Seoul Olympics.

## ❧ PREMIERSHIP TALK (8) ❧

"Young players need freedom of expression to develop as creative players... they should be encouraged to try skills without fear of failure."
*Arsenal manager Arsene Wenger*

# ✄ RYAN GIGGS, OBE ✄

Ryan Joseph Wilson was born in Cardiff on 29 November 1973. In July 1990 Ryan signed as a trainee with Manchester United, signing professional forms five months later. He then adopted his mother's maiden name and became Ryan Giggs. In March 1991 he made his first-team debut for United as a substitute against Everton at Old Trafford, and scored the winner against Manchester City on his full debut in May. His dazzling performances for United on their left wing earned him his first call-up to the Welsh national team in October 1991. Aged just 17 years and 321 days, he was at the time the youngest ever Welsh international.

In 1992–93, Ryan helped United to the inaugural FA Premier League Championship, the first of his ten championship-winners' medals. That season his peers voted him the PFA Young Player of the Year for the second season in succession – the award had never previously been won by the same player twice. The following season a dominant United won the domestic Double of Premier League and FA Cup; two years later they repeated the feat. A fourth Premiership-winners' medal followed in 1996–97, but Ryan's finest season was 1998–99, when United became the first and, to date, only winners of the Treble of League, FA Cup and Champions League. An outstanding memory from that campaign came when Ryan scored what is considered by many to be the greatest goal in FA Cup history, a thrilling zigzag run, in United's 2–1 win over Arsenal in the epic FA Cup semi-final replay at Villa Park. In November 1999 United won the Intercontinental Cup (World Club Championship) with a 1–0 win over Palmeiras of Brazil in Tokyo and Ryan took home a brand-new Toyota Celica car after being named Man of the Match.

On 23 August 2002, he scored his 100th goal for United in their 2–2 draw with Chelsea at Stamford Bridge. In May 2004, he collected his fourth FA Cup-winners' medal following United's 3–0 victory over Millwall in the Millennium Stadium, Cardiff. Giggsy played for his country 64 times and ended his international career captaining Wales in a 0–0 draw with the Czech Republic in a Euro 2008 qualifying game at the Millennium Stadium. On 11 May 2008, the day Giggs tied Sir Bobby Charlton's United appearance record with 758, he scored the decisive second goal in the title-winning match against Wigan Athletic.

No player in English football can boast Ryan's club trophy haul: ten Premiership crowns, four FA Cups, the League Cup twice, the UEFA Champions League twice and the European Cup Winners' Cup.

*Did You Know That?*
Ryan captained the England Schoolboys.

## ☒ THERE'S ONLY ONE DAVID BETNLEY ☒

When England international David Bentley took to the Old Trafford pitch for Blackburn Rovers' Premiership game against Manchester United on 11 November 2007 his name was spelt wrongly on the back of his shirt. Someone at the Ewood Park print shop had spelt his name BETNLEY. During the game itself, Manchester United beat Blackburn Rovers 2–0 to return to the top of the Premiership.

## ☒ A COSTLY BUNG ☒

On 21 February 1995, George Graham, who had been in charge of Arsenal for nine years and guided them to two First Division championships, was sacked by the London club after it was discovered that he had accepted an illegal "bung" of £425,000 from a Norwegian football agent, Rune Hauge, when Arsenal purchased John Jensen and Pal Lydersen after the 1992 European Championships. Graham, a former Arsenal and Manchester United player, was also handed a one-year ban from the game by the Football Association after he admitted to accepting an "unsolicited gift". The Gunners appointed Stewart Houston as their caretaker manager until the end of the season, after which Bruce Rioch took over.

## ☒ DOUBLE FOR GIGGSY ☒

Ryan Giggs, aged 19, was named the PFA Young Player of the Year in the 1992–93 season for the second successive year. Paul McGrath (Aston Villa), aged 34, was voted the PFA Players' Player of the Year, while 32-year-old Chris Waddle of Sheffield Wednesday collected the Football Writers' Player of the Year award.

## ☒ GOLDEN BALLS JOINS *LOS GALACTICOS* ☒

At the end of the 2002–03 season the newly crowned Premier League champions Manchester United sold one of their most prized assets, the England captain David Beckham. David, nicknamed "Golden Balls", joined Real Madrid, nicknamed *los galacticos*, for a staggering £25 million.

## ☒ SEVEN TO SEVEN ☒

In the 1993–94 Premiership season, Sheffield Wednesday finished in seventh place for the second successive year.

## ❧ FINAL PREMIERSHIP TABLE 1997–98 ❧

| Pos Team | P | W | D | L | F | A | Pts |
|---|---|---|---|---|---|---|---|
| 1. Arsenal (C) | 38 | 23 | 9 | 6 | 68 | 33 | 78 |
| 2. Manchester United | 38 | 23 | 8 | 7 | 73 | 26 | 77 |
| 3. Liverpool | 38 | 18 | 11 | 9 | 68 | 42 | 65 |
| 4. Chelsea | 38 | 20 | 3 | 15 | 71 | 43 | 63 |
| 5. Leeds United | 38 | 17 | 8 | 13 | 57 | 46 | 59 |
| 6. Blackburn Rovers | 38 | 16 | 10 | 12 | 57 | 52 | 58 |
| 7. Aston Villa | 38 | 17 | 6 | 15 | 49 | 48 | 57 |
| 8. West Ham United | 38 | 16 | 8 | 14 | 56 | 57 | 56 |
| 9. Derby County | 38 | 16 | 7 | 15 | 52 | 49 | 55 |
| 10. Leicester City | 38 | 13 | 14 | 11 | 51 | 41 | 53 |
| 11. Coventry City | 38 | 12 | 16 | 10 | 46 | 44 | 52 |
| 12. Southampton | 38 | 14 | 6 | 18 | 50 | 55 | 48 |
| 13. Newcastle United | 38 | 11 | 11 | 16 | 35 | 44 | 44 |
| 14. Tottenham Hotspur | 38 | 11 | 11 | 16 | 44 | 56 | 44 |
| 15. Wimbledon | 38 | 10 | 14 | 14 | 34 | 46 | 44 |
| 16. Sheffield Wednesday | 38 | 12 | 8 | 18 | 52 | 67 | 44 |
| 17. Everton | 38 | 9 | 13 | 16 | 41 | 56 | 40 |
| 18. Bolton Wanderers (R) | 38 | 9 | 13 | 16 | 41 | 61 | 40 |
| 19. Barnsley (R) | 38 | 10 | 5 | 23 | 37 | 82 | 35 |
| 20. Crystal Palace (R) | 38 | 8 | 9 | 21 | 37 | 71 | 33 |

## ❧ ERIKSSON ENDS GOAL DROUGHT ❧

In Sven-Goran Eriksson's first home game in charge of Manchester City, against Derby County on 15 August 2007, the team won 1–0 but, more importantly, Michael Johnson's winner ended a 227-day goal drought for City at home.

## ❧ NEW BACKERS ❧

From the beginning of the 1993-94 season the Premier League was sponsored by Carling Breweries and was officially named the FA Carling Premier League.

## ❧ EUROPEAN ROVERS ❧

For the second successive season Blackburn Rovers qualified for the UEFA Cup thanks to a sixth-place finish in the 2002–03 Premier League table. In season 2001–02 they qualified for the UEFA Cup as League Cup winners.

## ❧ A RECORD TUMBLES ❧

Derby County could only manage one win from their 38 Premiership games in the 2007–08 season – 1–0 at home to Newcastle United on 17 September – and ended up with 11 points, the lowest ever in the Premier League's 16-year history. Amazingly, the Rams finished 25 points from safety and a staggering 76 adrift of the Premiership winners, Manchester United. The previous record, set by Sunderland in 2005–06, was 15 points.

## ❧ BIG OGGI HANGS UP HIS GLOVES ❧

At the end of the 1999–2000 season Coventry City's goalkeeper, Steve Ogrizovic, retired from the game after 17 years with the club and 24 years as a professional footballer. Forty-three-year-old Ogrizovic was the last surviving member of Coventry's famous 1987 FA Cup-winning side still at Highfield Road. Steve holds the club record at Coventry City for the most appearances as a player with 601 in all competitions (504 league games) and is one of a select band of goalkeepers who have scored a goal directly from a goal-kick (in a 2–2 draw at Sheffield Wednesday on 12 October 1986).

## ❧ THE WEMBLEY OF THE NORTH ❧

At the end of the 1994–95 season, Leeds United finished fifth in the Premiership and announced ambitious new plans to build a new 65,000 all-seater stadium they dubbed "The Wembley of the North". The plans never came to fruition.

## ❧ CHANGES AT THE HELM ❧

In the summer of 1995 Arsenal appointed Bruce Rioch as their new manager. Rioch had just taken Bolton Wanderers into the Premiership after a 15-year exile from of the top flight. Bolton, meanwhile, appointed Roy McFarland and Colin Todd as joint managers, but McFarland was sacked on New Year's Day 1996, leaving Todd in sole charge. Alan Ball took charge at Manchester City, while David Pleat (Luton Town) replaced Trevor Francis at Sheffield Wednesday.

## ❧ ARSENAL'S UNWANTED DOUBLE ❧

In season 1999–2000 Arsenal finished runners-up to Manchester United in the Premiership for the second season running.

# ❧ PREMIERSHIP THREATENS ENGLAND ❧

In an interview with BBC1's *Inside Sport* programme on 3 September 2007, Sir Trevor Brooking, the Football Association's director of development, said that England's chances of achieving success on the pitch were in jeopardy. The former West Ham United and England international cited the influx of foreign players into the Premier League as the primary reason why England lack experienced players in key areas.

Sir Trevor said, "I don't think you can underestimate it. It's a major concern. Last year about 40 per cent of starting XIs in the Premier League were English. And with all the buying that has gone on over the summer that will probably fall to under a third. Will there be first-team opportunities for some of our youngsters aged between 17 and 21? If you look at Italy when they won the last World Cup, I think they had over 70 per cent of their league made up of domestic players. Spain, France, Holland, they're all up there, too. Germany aren't much better than us, but we're the lowest. The more that goes down, and the pool of choice reduces, we must come under pressure. In ten years' time you don't want us just being pleased to qualify for tournaments"

Research by *Inside Sport* showed that:

* 76 per cent of the starting XIs that played on the first weekend of the inaugural Premier League season in 1992–93 were English compared with 37 per cent on the first weekend of the 2007–08 season.
* Only 10 per cent (23 players) of the starting XIs in 1992–93 were from outside the UK compared with 56 per cent (123) in 2007–08.
* After the opening four weekends of the 2007–08 Premier League season non-English players had scored 69 per cent of the 118 goals (including two of the three own goals).
* Of those 118 goals scored, only nine were scored by seven different English forwards.
* According to the latest Deloitte figures for disclosed transfer fees, spending by Premier League clubs rose from £333 million in 2006 to £531 million in 2007.
* More than 50 per cent of the money spent by Premier League clubs for the 2007–08 Premiership campaign was handed over to non-English clubs.

# ❧ GUNNERS' LUCKY 13 ❧

The Premier League title clinched by Arsenal in 2004 was their third Premiership crown and their 13th championship overall.

## ❧ ARSENAL'S MILLENNIUM MAN ❧

When Emmanuel Adebayor scored Arsenal's second goal in their 3–1 win over Reading at the Madejski Stadium on 12 November 2007, it was the Gunners' 1,000th Premier League goal. They were now one of only two clubs – along with Manchester United – to have scored 1,000 or more goals in the Premiership. The Red Devils were on 1,136 at the time, having reached their thousandth goal during the 2005–06 season.

## ❧ CAPTAIN MARVEL LEAVES CHAMPIONS ❧

Bryan Robson left the Double winners Manchester United at the end of the 1993–94 season to take up the post of player-manager at Middlesbrough in Division One. Robbo, or "Captain Marvel" as he was nicknamed by the United and England fans, had spent 13 years at Old Trafford and won just about every honour in the game, including two Premier League titles, three FA Cups, one League Cup, one European Cup Winners' Cup and the European Super Cup. Robson appointed his former United team-mate, Viv Anderson, as his assistant manager.

## ❧ THE GLASGOW CONNECTION ❧

On 13 March 2002, Everton sacked manager Walter Smith and replaced the former Glasgow Rangers manager with a former Glasgow Celtic player, David Moyes. Moyes left his post as manager of Preston North End to take the helm at Goodison Park and managed to steer the troubled club clear of relegation, finishing 15th in the table, 37 points behind their bitter rivals Liverpool, who finished runners-up to champions Arsenal.

## ❧ ABLETT DOUBLES UP ❧

Gary Ablett won an FA Cup-winners' medal with Liverpool in 1989 and repeated the achievement with Everton in 1995.

## ❧ CROSSING THE BITTER DIVIDE ❧

At the start of the 2001–02 season, Arsenal unveiled their new signing, Sol Campbell, who moved across London from rivals Tottenham Hotspur on a free transfer. Campbell helped the Gunners to the Double in his first season with the club.

## ☙ PREMIERSHIP TALK (9) ❧

"There were one or two stray passes and they were getting on players' backs. It's out of order. I don't think some of them can even spell football, let alone understand it. Away from home our fans are fantastic. But at home they have a few drinks and probably the prawn sandwiches, and they don't realize what's going on out on the pitch."

*Roy Keane after United's 1–0 win over Dynamo Kiev in the UEFA Champions League*

## ☙ ERIC'S KUNG-FU ATTACK ❧

On 25 January 1995, Manchester United visited the capital for a Premiership game against Crystal Palace at Selhurst Park. The game ended in a 1–1 draw, but what happened during the match had a profound effect on the final destination of the Premiership trophy for the 1994–95 season. Cantona, United's enigmatic French striker and the reigning PFA Players' Player of the Year, was sent off and was verbally abused by a home fan on his way to the dressing-rooms. The red mist descended and Eric jumped, kung-fu style, into the crowd and lashed out at the foul-mouthed Eagles fan. A huge furore followed, as well as criminal charges, resulting in Cantona being banned by the Premier League for eight months, fined £20,000 and sentenced to two weeks in prison, which was subsequently reduced to 120 hours' community service on appeal. Without the inspirational Cantona, United narrowly missed out on winning the domestic Double for the second season in a row and their third successive Premiership crown, finishing one point behind Blackburn Rovers, and losing 1–0 to Everton in the 1995 FA Cup final.

## ☙ TWO HISTORIC LIONS ❧

On 7 June 2006, Gareth Southgate was appointed Middlesbrough manager after Steve McClaren took up his new role as England coach. Southgate had been a Boro player from 2001 up until his new appointment. Prior to joining Boro, Southgate played for Aston Villa (1995–2001) and, on 7 October 2000, Southgate and his Villa team-mate Gareth Barry, became the only two players to have played in England's last-ever international at the old Wembley Stadium (a 1–0 loss to Germany) and in the last FA Cup final under the famous Twin Towers (Villa lost the 2000 FA Cup final 1–0 to Chelsea).

## ❧ A CENTURY AT THE WRONG END ❧

During the 1993–94 Premiership season, Swindon Town won just five games, drew 15 and lost 22 to make an immediate return to Division One. The Robins not only found it hard to score goals, managing only 47 from their 42 games, but leaked them like a tap at the back, conceding 100 goals. Also relegated were Oldham Athletic, who only avoided the drop the previous season on goal difference, and Sheffield United.

## ❧ THE £¼ BILLION TEAM ❧

The Chelsea team that won the 2004–05 Premier League Championship title was the most expensive football team ever created in the history of British football. The team cost an estimated £250 million to assemble and included star purchases such as Wayne Bridge, Ricardo Carvalho, Petr Cech, Joe Cole, Didier Drogba, Paulo Ferreira, Eidur Gudjohnsen, Frank Lampard and Claude Makele.

## ❧ THE SAINTS' MIRACLE WORKER ❧

In season 1997–98 Dave Jones, whose previous management experience had not seen him manage a team above Division Two, guided Southampton to a highly respectable 12th place in the final Premier League table.

## ❧ OLDEST PREMIER LEAGUE MANAGER ❧

In September 1999, Ruud Gullit quit his position as manager of Newcastle United after the Geordies lost four of their opening five Premiership games and was replaced by the former England manager Sir Bobby Robson. At the time Sir Bobby was 66 years old, making him the oldest manager in the history of the Premiership (he was 71 when he left the Geordies in 2004). Newcastle United finished the 1999–2000 season 11th in the table, four places below their bitter rivals Sunderland, who had only won promotion the previous season.

## ❧ PLAYERS PAY FOR FANS' TRAVEL ❧

On 24 November 2007, the Reading players subsidized their fans' trip to Manchester to see the team play Manchester City in the Premiership. The Royals squad donated £5,000 towards the costs of providing coaches to take fans to Eastlands. City won the match 2–1.

# LIVERPOOL PREMIER LEAGUE FANTASY XI

**1**
Bruce
*GROBBELAAR*

**2**
Steve
*FINNAN*

**6**
Sami
*HYYPIA*

**5**
Jamie
*CARRAGHER*

**3**
John Arne
*RIISE*

**7**
Steve
*McMANAMAN*

**4**
Xabi
*ALONSO*

**8**
Steven
*GERRARD*
(capt.)

**9**
Ian
*RUSH*

**10**
Robbie
*FOWLER*

**11**
John
*BARNES*

*Substitutes*
David *JAMES* • Fernando *TORRES* • Mark *WRIGHT*,
Jamie *REDKNAPP* • Michael *OWEN*
*Manager*
Gerard *HOULLIER* OBE

### Did You Know That?
Gerard Houllier was the manager of the French national side from
1992 to 1993.

## SIX APPEAL

Cristiano Ronaldo's first hat-trick for Manchester United helped
the champions to a comfortable 6–0 win over Newcastle United at
Old Trafford in the Premiership on 12 January 2008. Amazingly,
all six United goals came in the second half, when the managerless
Geordies were totally outclassed in all areas of the pitch.

## A BARN FULL OF OWLS

In October 1997, Sheffield Wednesday sacked their manager David
Pleat and brought in Ron Atkinson as caretaker manager. At the end
of the 1997–98 season, after guiding the Owls to 16th position and
Premiership safety, Big Ron was replaced with Barnsley's outgoing
manager Danny Wilson, a former Owls player.

## ❧ AN EARLY BATH ❧

Dave Kitson came on as a substitute for Reading against Manchester United at Old Trafford in their opening game of the 2007–08 season and was quickly given an early bath – it was the first Premiership sending-off of the season. The game ended 0–0.

## ❧ AN EXPENSIVE PAIR OF GLOVES ❧

Prior to the start of the 1993–94 season Tim Flowers became Britain's most expensive goalkeeper when he left Southampton to join Kenny Dalglish's Blackburn Rovers in a deal worth £2.5 million.

## ❧ SURVIVAL SUNDAY ❧

Sunday, 15 May 2005, was the last day of the 2004–05 Premiership season. West Bromwich Albion sat at the foot of the table, and the other two relegation places were occupied by Southampton and Crystal Palace, both precariously placed one point above the Baggies. Norwich City occupied the last safe spot, two points above the foot of the table. This final day of the Premierhip season was unique in that, for the first time in the league's 13-year history, no club had been assured of relegation Southampton lost 2–1 at home to Manchester United and were relegated. Norwich City, with their fate in their own hands, lost 6–0 to Fulham at Craven Cottage and also went down. Crystal Palace were leading 2–1 at Charlton Athletic, with just eight minutes separating them from Premiership survival. But they conceded an equalizer to Jonathan Fortune, which was enough to send the Eagles back to the Championship. Meanwhile West Bromwich Albion beat Portsmouth 2–0 at the Hawthorns to avoid the drop.

## ❧ TOP HAMMER ❧

Prior to the start of the 1994–95 season, West Ham United sacked manager and former hero Billy Bonds – their 1975 and 1980 FA Cup-winning captain. His replacement, Harry Redknapp, another former player, acted swiftly to deflect any flak coming his way by bringing Hammers hero Tony Cottee back to the Boleyn Ground from Everton after a six-year absence. Redknapp, who had been linked with a return to take charge of his old club Bournemouth, guided the London club to 14th in the Premiership.

# ❧ EVERTON PREMIER LEAGUE FANTASY XI ❧

**1**
Neville
*SOUTHALL*

**2**
Phil
*NEVILLE*

**6**
Joleon
*LESCOTT*

**5**
Dave
*WATSON*

**3**
David
*UNSWORTH*

**7**
Mikel
*ARTETA*

**4**
Thomas
*GRAVESON*

**8**
Anders
*LIMPAR*

**9**
Tim
*CAHILL*

**10**
Duncan
*FERGUSON*

**11**
Andy
*JOHNSON*

*Substitutes*
Tim *HOWARD* • Andy *HINCHCLIFFE* • Peter *BEAGRIE*,
Kevin *KILBANE* • *YAKUBU*
*Manager*
David *MOYES*

---

**Did You Know That?**

David Moyes had to pay a club record fee of £11.25 million to secure the services of Yakubu from Middlesbrough in the summer of 2007.

## ❧ WHEN THE GUNS FAILED TO FIRE ❧

The 1994–95 season was one of turmoil for Arsenal. George Graham was sacked over a bungs scandal and was temporarily replaced by Stewart Houston until Bruce Rioch came in at the end of the season. The Gunners, First Division winners in 1989 and 1991, could only manage 12th place in the Premiership. However, Arsenal did reach the final of the European Cup Winners' Cup for the second year in succession and faced Real Zaragoza in Paris. The game went into extra-time, and with 120 minutes shown on the game clock and the score at 1–1, a penalty shoot-out was beckoning when Nayim lobbed David Seaman from the half-way line to win the trophy for the Spaniards. To add insult to injury, Nayim, full name Mohammed Ali Amar, played for Tottenham Hotspur from 1988 to 1993.

## ❧ THE WAY IT USED TO BE ❧

Manchester United finished runners-up to Leeds United in the final season of the English First Division Championship in 1991–92, but their dominance of British football during the 1990s was just about to commence. Luton Town, Nottingham Forest and West Ham United were all relegated to the newly formed English League Division One, which replaced the former Second Division. During the season the legendary West Ham United and England captain, Bobby Moore, died of cancer aged just 51 (24 February 1993).

Ipswich Town, winners of the last-ever Second Division championship under the old system, and runners-up Middlesbrough, hit the jackpot with automatic promotion to the newly formed FA Premier League and a share of the money poured into it by BSkyB. Blackburn Rovers, managed by the legendary Glasgow Celtic, Liverpool and Scotland striker, Kenny Dalglish, won the play-off final 1–0 against Leicester City thanks to a goal from Mike Newell, a former Leicester City striker. Dalglish, backed by owner Sir Jack Walker's deep pockets, ended Rovers' 26-year absence from English football's top flight.

## ❧ BRUMMIES JOIN BLACK CATS IN THE DROP ❧

Birmingham City and West Bromwich Albion were relegated to the Coca-Cola League along with Sunderland at the end of the 2005–06 Premier League season.

## ❧ OLD BIG 'EAD ❧

In 1993 Nottingham Forest finished bottom of the inaugural FA Premier League and were relegated. Their run of six successive defeats during the season was the worst suffered by any of the Premiership's 22 clubs. It was a sad end to the Forest reign of Brian Clough, who took the decision to retire. When the man nicknamed "Old Big 'ead" took charge at the City Ground, in January 1975, Forest were a mediocre Division Two side who still looked on their two FA Cup final wins (in 1898 and 1959) as the defining moments in the club's history. Cloughie rewrote their history books, guiding them to the First Division championship in 1978, European Cup success in 1979 and again in 1980, as well as four League Cups. All but two of Forest's trophies under Clough (two League Cups) came during his first six years at the helm.

## ⚜ FINAL PREMIERSHIP TABLE 1998–99 ⚜

| Pos Team | P | W | D | L | F | A | Pts |
|---|---|---|---|---|---|---|---|
| 1. Manchester United (C) | 38 | 22 | 13 | 3 | 80 | 37 | 79 |
| 2. Arsenal | 38 | 22 | 12 | 4 | 59 | 17 | 78 |
| 3. Chelsea | 38 | 20 | 15 | 3 | 57 | 30 | 75 |
| 4. Leeds United | 38 | 18 | 13 | 7 | 62 | 34 | 67 |
| 5. West Ham United | 38 | 16 | 9 | 13 | 46 | 53 | 57 |
| 6. Aston Villa | 38 | 15 | 10 | 13 | 55 | 51 | 55 |
| 7. Liverpool | 38 | 15 | 9 | 14 | 68 | 49 | 54 |
| 8. Derby County | 38 | 13 | 13 | 12 | 40 | 45 | 52 |
| 9. Middlesbrough | 38 | 12 | 15 | 11 | 48 | 54 | 51 |
| 10. Leicester City | 38 | 12 | 13 | 13 | 40 | 46 | 49 |
| 11. Tottenham Hotspur | 38 | 11 | 14 | 13 | 47 | 50 | 47 |
| 12. Sheffield Wednesday | 38 | 13 | 7 | 18 | 41 | 42 | 46 |
| 13. Newcastle United | 38 | 11 | 13 | 14 | 48 | 54 | 46 |
| 14. Everton | 38 | 11 | 10 | 17 | 42 | 47 | 43 |
| 15. Coventry City | 38 | 11 | 9 | 18 | 39 | 51 | 42 |
| 16. Wimbledon | 38 | 10 | 12 | 16 | 40 | 63 | 42 |
| 17. Southampton | 38 | 11 | 8 | 19 | 37 | 64 | 41 |
| 18. Charlton Athletic (R) | 38 | 8 | 12 | 18 | 41 | 56 | 36 |
| 19. Blackburn Rovers (R) | 38 | 7 | 14 | 17 | 38 | 52 | 35 |
| 20. Nottingham Forest (R) | 38 | 7 | 9 | 22 | 35 | 69 | 30 |

## ⚜ TOP CANARY ⚜

At the start of the 1992–93 season, Norwich City youth team manager Mike Walker was promoted to the hot seat in place of Dave Stringer. Under Walker's guidance the Canaries made it to third place in the league and into European football in the shape of the UEFA Cup for the 1993–94 season. It would be the Canaries' first experience of European football. Eight years earlier their 1–0 win over Sunderland in the 1984–85 League Cup final guaranteed the club UEFA Cup football in the 1985–86 season. However, following the Heysel tragedy in May 1985, English clubs were banned from Europe and the Canaries missed out on their inaugural European adventure.

## ⚜ DEN BREAKS BANK ⚜

When Dennis Bergkamp joined Arsenal from Inter Milan for £7.5 million in June 1995, the fee was a new British transfer record. Bruce Rioch, the Arsenal manager, also paid close to £5 million to Sampdoria for the services of the England captain David Platt.

## ❧ AU REVOIR, CANTONA ❧

On 18 May 1997, the day after Manchester United were crowned Premiership champions for 1996–97, Eric Cantona dropped a bombshell on the club by announcing his retirement from playing. The enigmatic French maestro joined United in November 1992 from Leeds United for a modest £1.1 million and over the next five seasons he helped Manchester United win four Premiership titles (1992–93, 1993–94, 1995–96 and 1996–97) and two FA Cups (1994 and 1996) as well being voted PFA Player of the Year in 1994 and FWA Player of the Year in 1996. His departure left United fans everywhere heartbroken.

## ❧ CHAMPIONS LEAGUE BECKONING ❧

Four games into the 2007–08 Premier League season Wigan Athletic found themselves sitting third in the table – which as a final league position would be enough to secure entry to the third qualifying round of the 2008–09 UEFA Champions League campaign.

## ❧ LATICS GET THEIR MAN AGAIN ❧

On 19 November 2007, Steve Bruce packed his bags as manager of Birmingham City after almost six years in charge at St Andrews to take up the managerial reins at Wigan Athletic. It was the second time the former Manchester United captain managed the Latics, having been their boss for seven weeks in 2001. Dave Whelan, the chairman of Wigan Athletic, agreed to pay Birmingham City £3 million in compensation for Bruce's services. Bruce succeeded Chris Hutchings, who was sacked at the beginning of November 2007.

## ❧ FROM APPRENTICE TO SORCERER ❧

In early October 1998, George Graham resigned as the Leeds United manager to become Tottenham Hotspur's new boss, after the London club had sacked Christian Gross. Leicester City manager Martin O'Neill was hotly tipped to take charge of the Yorkshire club, but he stayed loyal to the Foxes. Instead, another Irishman, David O'Leary, was promoted from Leeds' assistant manager into the hot seat. While Graham went on to guide Spurs to League Cup glory in 1999, O'Leary steered Leeds to fourth place in the Premiership, and both clubs were guaranteed UEFA Cup football in the 1999–2000 season.

## ⚜ PREMIERSHIP TALK (10) ⚜

"It was a freakish incident. If I tried it 100 or a million times it couldn't happen again. If I could I would have carried on playing!"
*Sir Alex Ferguson on how he kicked a boot that hit David Beckham above his eye*

## ⚜ RETURN OF THE TOON KING ⚜

On 16 January 2008, Newcastle United announced that former player and former manager Kevin Keegan would make a dramatic return to manage the Magpies. The 56-year-old former England, Newcastle United, Fulham and Manchester City boss, who managed the Geordies from 1992 to 1997, made a hero's return to St James' Park as the successor to Sam Allardyce.

## ⚜ THE KID FROM OZ ⚜

In season 1999–2000 Leeds United's exciting young Australian midfielder, Harry Kewell, helped the Elland Road club to a third-place finish in the Premiership table and UEFA Champions League football the following season. Kewell's performances throughout the season earned him the PFA Young Player of the Year Award.

## ⚜ THE LAST MAINE ROAD DERBY ⚜

In the 2002–03 season, Manchester City beat Manchester United 3–1 at Maine Road in what was the last ever Manchester derby game played at Maine Road. It was also City's first win over the red half of Manchester in 13 years, during which time United had collected seven Premiership crowns. However, despite the 3–1 defeat, United went on to lift their eighth Premiership title at the end of the campaign. City in contrast finished ninth in the Premiership table and moved to their new home at Eastlands (the City of Manchester Stadium) for the start of the new season.

## ⚜ TOFFEE GAZZA ⚜

At the end of the 1999–2000 season Everton finished a disappointing 13th in the Premiership table, leading their manager Walter Smith to turn to one of his former players at Rangers to help bring the good times back to Goodison Park. Over the close season Smith managed to persuade Paul Gascoigne to leave Middlesbrough for Everton.

# ⚽ TOP-PRICE PREMIERSHIP SEATS IN 2007–08 ⚽

The following table lists the prices of the most expensive adult seats – from the most expensive to the cheapest – at all the Premiership clubs during the 2007–08 season.

| Team | Stadium | £ |
|---|---|---|
| Arsenal | Emirates Stadium | 94 |
| Tottenham Hotspur | White Hart Lane | 71 |
| Chelsea | Stamford Bridge | 66 |
| West Ham United | Upton Park | 61 |
| Newcastle United | St James' Park | 60 |
| Sunderland | Stadium of Light | 55 |
| Fulham | Craven Cottage | 50 |
| Birmingham City | St Andrews | 48 |
| Derby County | Pride Park | 44 |
| Manchester United | Old Trafford | 44 |
| Portsmouth | Fratton Park | 41 |
| Reading | Madejski Stadium | 41 |
| Middlesbrough | Riverside Stadium | 40 |
| Bolton Wanderers | Reebok Stadium | 39 |
| Liverpool | Anfield | 36 |
| Manchester City | Eastlands | 36 |
| Aston Villa | Villa Park | 35 |
| Blackburn Rovers | Ewood Park | 35 |
| Everton | Goodison Park | 34 |
| Wigan Athletic | JJB Stadium | 25 |

## ⚽ THE BOYS ARE BACK IN TOWN ⚽

Going into the 2004–05 season Crystal Palace and Norwich City were back among the big boys after winning promotion from the Championship, along with Premier League newcomers West Bromwich Albion.

## ⚽ CRAZY GANG DEFY THE ODDS ⚽

In season 1993–94 Wimbledon, the least wealthy of all the clubs in the Premier League and a team who didn't even have a home ground (they were still renting Crystal Palace's Selhurst Park), defied the odds and finished sixth in the table to equal their highest-ever finish in the top flight. Only one London club, Arsenal (fourth), finished above the Crazy Gang.

# ⚑ THIERRY HENRY ⚑

Thierry Daniel Henry was born in Les Ulis, Essonne, a suburb of Paris, on 17 August 1977. When he was 12 years old, a scout from AS Monaco watched him score six goals in a match that his team won 6–0 and immediately signed him without even a trial. From 1990 to 1992 he was loaned out to Viry-Chatillon to gain experience, and in 1992 he also attended Clairefontaine, the French national football centre of excellence. Two years later he made his professional debut for AS Monaco, and in 1997 he made his international debut for France. During his four years in the first team at AS Monaco he scored 20 goals in 110 matches in Le Championnat, winning a league title in 1996–97. It was enough to convince the Italian giants Juventus to buy him. However, his move to Serie A did not work out, as he was usually played out of position on the right wing. In 1999 Arsene Wenger, his former manager at AS Monaco, paid £10.5 million to bring him to Arsenal as a replacement for Nicolas Anelka, who had moved on to Real Madrid.

Although Henry failed to score in his first eight games, he soon flourished in Wenger's side. In his first season with Arsenal he scored 26 goals, with the team finishing runners-up to Manchester United in the Premier League and beaten finalists in the UEFA Cup to Galatasaray. In the summer of 2000 Henry was one of a number of star French players who helped their country to victory in the European Championships. After Arsenal had finished runners-up to Manchester United in the Premiership for the third consecutive year in 2000–01, Henry's 32 goals helped the Gunners to complete the Double of Premier League and FA Cup success in season 2001–02.

In season 2002–03 Henry banged in 43 goals in all competitions for Arsenal as they retained the FA Cup. Although United reclaimed the Premiership crown, Henry collected the PFA Players' Player of the Year Award and the Football Writers' Association Footballer of the Year Award. Season 2003–04 saw Arsenal not only win back the Premiership title but also go through the entire season unbeaten, and following Patrick Vieira's departure to Juventus in 2005 Henry was made club captain. Henry led Arsenal to the UEFA Champions League final in 2006, but a year later he left for FC Barcelona, their conquerors in the final.

### Did You Know That?

Thierry Henry surpassed the club's all-time goalscoring record set by Cliff Bastin, scoring 226 goals in all competitions for the Gunners.

## ॐ 125-UP FOR SPURS ॐ

The 2007–08 season was Tottenham Hotspur's 125th year of existence.

## ॐ THE UNDEFEATED CHAMPIONS ॐ

Arsenal, Premiership champions for the third time in season 2003–04, went through their entire league campaign of 38 matches unbeaten, matching the feat of Preston North End in 1888–89. Arsenal finished the Premiership campaign with 26 wins, 12 draws and 90 points. In 1888–89 the Lilywhites of Preston, playing in the inaugural First Division championship, ended their league campaign with 18 wins, 4 draws and 40 points (under the 2 points for a win system).

## ॐ THOSE EUROPEAN BLUES ॐ

In season 2002–03 Chelsea finished fourth in the Premier League table, 16 points behind the champions Manchester United, and qualified for the UEFA Champions League the following season. It was the Blues' first UEFA Champions League qualification in five seasons. Back in 1955 Chelsea won the First Division and were invited to participate in the inaugural European Cup. However, the Football Association barred them from entering the competition.

## ॐ OUT OF AFRICA ॐ

On 17 January, just three days before the 2008 African Cup of Nations kicked off in Ghana, FIFA president Sepp Blatter said that the timing of the Africa Cup of Nations must be changed. Blatter said that by 2016 the biennial tournament must be held in June and July, like other major tournaments, and many Premiership managers backed his call. Since 2002 the exodus of Premier League players to play in the biennial tournament has seen a steady increase:

| Year | Hosts | No. of Premier League players called up |
|------|-------|----------------------------------------|
| 2002 | Mali | 8 |
| 2004 | Tunisia | 18 |
| 2006 | Egypt | 22 |
| 2008 | Ghana | 35 |

## ❧ THE CHELSEA JINX ❧

On 26 November 2007 Billy Davies became the sixth Premiership manager of the 2007–08 season to lose his job when he left Derby County. Davies left the Rams rooted to the foot of the table, two points adrift of the club in 19th place, following their 2–0 home defeat to Chelsea. Amazingly, two of the other five Premier League managers, Sammy Lee (Bolton Wanderers) and Chris Hutchings (Wigan Athletic), also lost their jobs after losing to Chelsea. Another former Wigan Athletic manager, Paul Jewell, took charge of Derby.

## ❧ THE FOREIGN INVASION BEGINS ❧

Prior to the start of the 1995–96 season, the Nottingham Forest manager Frank Clark signed Andrea Silenzi from AS Torino for £1.8 million, and he became the first Italian ever to play in the English Premier League. Silenzi failed to settle, however, making just ten league appearances without scoring. Two games into the 1996–97 season Forest loaned the Italian out to Venezia, and after making a further ten appearances for Forest (seven starts), scoring twice, he moved on to Reggina in the summer of 1997.

## ❧ A MAN OF MANY AWARDS ❧

In addition to being the Premier League's highest-ever goalscorer with 260 career goals (112 with Blackburn Rovers and 148 with Newcastle United), Alan Shearer is Newcastle United's all-time leading goalscorer with 206 from 404 games (1996–97 to 2005–06). He also holds the Geordies' European goals record with 30 and was the leading goalscorer for his club for ten seasons: Blackburn Rovers 1994–95 and 1995–96, Newcastle United 1996–97, 1998–99, 1999–2000, 2001–02, 2002–03, 2003–04, 2004–05 and 2005–06. Alan was inducted into the English Football Hall of Fame in 2004 and is named in FIFA's list of the "100 Greatest Living Footballers". He was also named as the Overall Player of the Decade and the Domestic Player of the Decade when the Premier League held an awards ceremony to celebrate the first ten years of the Premiership (1992–93 to 2001–02).

## ❧ POMPEY'S 12TH MAN ❧

Portsmouth retired the No. 12 shirt in honour of their fans, their "12th man on the pitch".

# ❧ SPURS PREMIER LEAGUE FANTASY XI ❧

**1**
Paul
*ROBINSON*

**2**
Stephen
*CARR*

**6**
Sol
*CAMPBELL*

**5**
Ledley
*KING*
*(capt)*

**3**
Justin
*EDINBURGH*

**7**
Aaron
*LENNON*

**4**
Jermaine
*JENAS*

**8**
Gus
*POYET*

**10**
Jurgen
*KLINSMANN*

**9**
Dimitar
*BERBATOV*

**11**
Robbie
*KEANE*

*Substitutes*
Ian *WALKER* • Garry *MABBUTT* • Darren *ANDERTON* •
Teddy *SHERINGHAM* • Jermaine *DEFOE*
*Manager*
Martin *JOL*

### *Did You Know That?*
On December 26, 2007, Robbie Keane became only the 13th player
in the history of the league to score 100 Premiership goals

## ❧ MANAGERIAL MUSICAL CHAIRS ❧

In November 1994 Gerry Francis left Queen's Park Rangers and
became the new boss of Tottenham Hotspur. Ray Wilkins, who had
left Loftus Road in February 1995 to take up the position of player-
coach at Crystal Palace, returned to QPR as player-manager. Spurs
ended the season seventh in the Premiership with QPR just two
points and one place below them in eighth position.

## ❧ THE CUNNING FOXES ❧

In their first season in the Premiership, 1996–97, Martin O'Neill
guided Leicester City to an impressive ninth place, while the Foxes
also beat Middlesbrough in the 1997 League Cup final at Wembley.

## ❧ MARCH MADNESS FOR ERIC ❧

Manchester United's Eric Cantona became the first player to be sent off in consecutive Premier League games. On 19 March 1994, the enigmatic Frenchman was dismissed after stamping on Swindon Town's John Moncur during United's 2–2 draw at the County Ground. Three days later, Cantona was given an early bath at Highbury in United's 2–2 draw with the Gunners, although this decision was somewhat harsh. Despite his double whammy, Cantona scored 25 times for the champions over the course of the season, helped the Reds to the domestic Double and their second successive Premiership crown, and was voted the PFA Player of the Year.

## ❧ UNLUCKY 13 FOR RANGERS ❧

After enjoying 13 years among the big boys, Queen's Park Rangers lost their top-flight status in 1995–96 when they finished the season second from bottom of the Premiership. The loss of Les Ferdinand, sold to Newcastle United for £6 million, was one of the major factors for the London side's poor season.

## ❧ LE GOD RETIRES ❧

A terrible start to the 2001–02 season cost Southampton manager Stuart Gray the sack less than six months after he took charge at St Mary's. Gordon Strachan, who had left Coventry City, was appointed as Gray's successor and steered the Saints to an 11th-place finish in the table. It was the last season at Southampton for Matthew Le Tissier, nicknamed "Le God" by the Southampton fans, as he took the decision to hang up his boots after 16 years of loyal service to the Saints. However, Le Tissier was kept on by Strachan as a coach at St Mary's.

## ❧ JOB CUTS ON MERSEYSIDE ❧

In December 1993, Howard Kendall's second spell in charge of Everton ended when he resigned and walked out of Goodison Park. All was not well on the other side of Stanley Park either, and a month later Liverpool sacked Graeme Souness after losing at home to Bristol City in the third round of the FA Cup. Everton replaced Kendall with Norwich City boss Mike Walker, and their neighbours promoted coach Roy Evans to manager. John Deehan took over from Mike Walker at Carrow Road.

## OL' BLUE EYES IS BACK IN TOWN

On 6 July 2007, Manchester City announced that Sven-Goran Eriksson had been appointed manager in place of Stuart Pearce. The former England coach guided City to wins in their opening three games, including a 1–0 win over Manchester United in the Manchester derby, to send City to the top of the Premier League.

## REDS CONTINUE HOT STREAK

Manchester United finished runners-up to Arsenal in season 1997–98, which meant that since the Premier League began in 1992–93 the Red Devils had never finished below runners-up position (four wins, two second places). Meanwhile Arsenal became the third different team to win the Premiership title after United (1992–93, 1993–94, 1995–96 & 1996–97) and Blackburn Rovers (1994–95).

## AL PLAYS THE TOON

At the end of the 1995–96 season Alan Shearer left Blackburn Rovers and signed for Newcastle United for a world-record transfer fee of £15 million.

## KEEGAN TURNS BLUE

When Manchester City sacked Joe Royle at the end of the 2000–01 season following the club's relegation to Division One, they brought in the former England manager Kevin Keegan to try and win promotion back into the Premier League. Keegan had resigned as the coach of England on 7 October 2000 shortly after his team lost 1–0 at home to Germany in their opening 2002 World Cup qualifying game.

## NAMED AND NUMBERED

At the start of the 1993–94 season the Premier League introduced squad numbers for England's top-flight clubs.

## PREMIERSHIP TALK (11)

"I would love an Aston Martin but if you ask me £1m for an Aston Martin, I tell you, you are crazy because they cost £250,000."
*Former Chelsea manager Jose Mourinho*

## ❧ FINAL PREMIERSHIP TABLE 1999–2000 ❧

| Pos | Team | P | W | D | L | F | A | Pts |
|---|---|---|---|---|---|---|---|---|
| 1. | Manchester United (C) | 38 | 28 | 7 | 3 | 97 | 45 | 91 |
| 2. | Arsenal | 38 | 22 | 7 | 9 | 73 | 43 | 73 |
| 3. | Leeds United | 38 | 21 | 6 | 11 | 58 | 43 | 69 |
| 4. | Liverpool | 38 | 19 | 10 | 9 | 51 | 30 | 67 |
| 5. | Chelsea | 38 | 18 | 11 | 9 | 53 | 34 | 65 |
| 6. | Aston Villa | 38 | 15 | 13 | 10 | 46 | 35 | 58 |
| 7. | Sunderland | 38 | 16 | 10 | 12 | 57 | 56 | 58 |
| 8. | Leicester City | 38 | 16 | 7 | 15 | 55 | 55 | 55 |
| 9. | West Ham United | 38 | 15 | 10 | 13 | 52 | 53 | 55 |
| 10. | Tottenham Hotspur | 38 | 15 | 8 | 15 | 57 | 49 | 53 |
| 11. | Newcastle United | 38 | 14 | 10 | 14 | 63 | 54 | 52 |
| 12. | Middlesbrough | 38 | 14 | 10 | 14 | 46 | 52 | 52 |
| 13. | Everton | 38 | 12 | 14 | 12 | 59 | 49 | 50 |
| 14. | Coventry City | 38 | 12 | 8 | 18 | 47 | 54 | 44 |
| 15. | Southampton | 38 | 12 | 8 | 18 | 45 | 62 | 44 |
| 16. | Derby County | 38 | 9 | 11 | 18 | 44 | 57 | 38 |
| 17. | Bradford City | 38 | 9 | 9 | 20 | 38 | 68 | 36 |
| 18. | Wimbledon (R) | 38 | 7 | 12 | 19 | 46 | 74 | 33 |
| 19. | Sheffield Wednesday (R) | 38 | 8 | 7 | 23 | 38 | 70 | 31 |
| 20. | Watford (R) | 38 | 6 | 6 | 26 | 35 | 77 | 24 |

## ❧ NO WAY PAST ❧

At the end of the 2007–08 season, England international goalkeeper David James held the record for keeping the highest number of clean sheets in the Premier League with 159. James, who was also the first goalkeeper to make 500 appearances in the Premier League, left Watford to join Liverpool in 1992 and he has played in the Premiership for the Reds, Aston Villa, West Ham United, Manchester City and Portsmouth. On the flip side, James, who played in the first ever Premier League match televised live, has also conceded the most number of goals in Premiership history.

Petr Cech holds the Premiership record for the most clean sheets in a single season, having notched up an impressive 24 shut-outs for Chelsea in 2004–05. Cech also holds the English league record for the longest period of time without conceding a goal, a staggering 1,025 minutes playing for Chelsea in 2004–05.

Pepe Reina of Liverpool has kept the most clean sheets in all three of his seasons in the Premiership. In 2007–08, opponents failed to score in 18 of the 38 matches the ever-present Reina played.

## ❧ THE PREMIERSHIP SIX ❧

Of the teams that have played at least one season in the Premier League there are six that do not share their last name with any of the other 92 clubs in the Premier League and Football League: Aston Villa, Nottingham Forest, Tottenham Hotspur, Crystal Palace, Queen's Park Rangers and Sheffield Wednesday. In total there are 14 such teams among the 92, the others being: Crewe Alexandra, Plymouth Argyle, AFC Bournemouth, MK Dons, Preston North End, Leyton Orient, Accrington Stanley and Port Vale.

## ❧ STEPPING INTO THE LIGHT ❧

At the end of the 1995–96 season Peter Reid guided Sunderland to First Division championship glory and Premiership football in season 1996–97. Meanwhile Jim Smith helped Derby County win promotion to the Premiership and Martin O'Neill secured his third promotion in four seasons by taking Leicester City into the Premier League via the First Division play-offs.

## ❧ WE WANT OUR TROPHY BACK ❧

During the summer of 1998, after United finished runners-up to Arsenal in season 1997–98, Alex Ferguson raided Manchester United's coffers and broke the club's record transfer fee twice in his bid to put United back on top, where all their fans felt they belonged. To replace Gary Pallister, who had left the club, Fergie splashed out £10.75 million to secure the services of the 25-year-old Dutch centre-back Jaap Stam. Then he swooped for Aston Villa's Trinidad & Tobago international striker Dwight Yorke, for whom he paid £12.6 million. Fergie rounded off his summer spending with the £5m acquisition of the Swedish international winger Jesper Blomqvist from Parma. The spending worked as United won the Treble.

## ❧ THE RETURN OF THE INCREDIBLE SULK ❧

Five years after finishing joint fourth in the Premier League goalscoring table with 17 goals for Arsenal in the 1998–99 season, Nicolas Anelka again finished joint fourth in season 2003–04, and again with 17 goals, but this time as a Manchester City player. Anelka was Manchester City's record purchase when Kevin Keegan signed him from Paris Saint-Germain in the summer of 2002 for £12 million.

## ❧ CAT'S NINE LIVES ❧

On 24 August 2007, Sunderland manager Roy Keane signed his former Manchester United team-mate Andy Cole. Sunderland was Cole's eighth Premiership club, following spells at Newcastle United, Manchester United, Blackburn Rovers, Fulham, Manchester City, Birmingham City and Portsmouth (while on loan from Birmingham). He actually began his career at Arsenal in pre-Premiership days and went out on loan to both Fulham and Bristol City, before making the move to Ashton Gate permanent.

## ❧ UNITED BUST BANK TWICE ❧

At the end of the 2000–01 season, champions Manchester United broke their own club record transfer fee twice. The first signing was the Dutch international striker Ruud van Nistelrooy, for whom United paid PSV Eindhoven a cool £19 million. This was followed by a whopping £28.1 million for Lazio's Argentine midfielder Juan Sebastian Veron. At the time Veron was the most expensive footballer in the history of British football.

## ❧ WHEN FIFTH BECOMES FIRST ❧

Despite Sir Alex Ferguson leading Manchester United to their third consecutive Premiership title in 2001, their seventh in nine years, the Manager of the Year Award went to Ipswich Town's George Burley. The Suffolk club finished fifth in the table, above clubs with far greater resources, including Chelsea (sixth), Aston Villa (eighth), Newcastle United (tenth), Tottenham Hotspur (11th) and Everton (16th).

## ❧ BANGING THEM IN ❧

Newcastle star striker Alan Shearer finished as the Premiership's top goalscorer in season 1996–97, with 25 goals in 31 games.

## ❧ NO CHEER FOR SPARKY ❧

On their way to securing their second domestic Double in 1995–96 Manchester United beat Chelsea 2–1 at Villa Park in the FA Cup semi-final. Mark "Sparky" Hughes was in the Chelsea team that lost to the rampant Red Devils. Ironically, he had scored for the Reds in their 4–0 FA Cup final win over the Blues in 1994 when United claimed their first Double success.

# ❧ ENGLAND PREMIER LEAGUE FANTASY XI ❧

**1**
David
*SEAMAN*
(ARSENAL & MAN CITY)

**2**
Gary
*NEVILLE*
(MANCHESTER UTD)

**6**
Tony
*ADAMS*
(ARSENAL, capt.)

**5**
Rio
*FERDINAND*
(WEST HAM, LEEDS & MAN UTD)

**3**
Stuart
*PEARCE*
(NOTTINGHAM FOR. & WEST HAM)

**7**
David
*BECKHAM*
(MANCHESTER UTD)

**4**
Steven
*GERRARD*
(LIVERPOOL)

**11**
John
*BARNES*
(LIVERPOOL, NEWCASTLE & CHARLTON)

**9**
Michael
*OWEN*
(LIVERPOOL, & NEWCASTLE)

**10**
Alan
*SHEARER*
(SOUTHAMPTON, BLACKBURN & NEWCASTLE)

**8**
Wayne
*ROONEY*
(EVERTON & MAN UTD)

*Substitutes*

Tim *FLOWERS* (*Southampton, Blackburn & Leicester*) • John *TERRY* (*Chelsea*)
Ashley *COLE* (*Arsenal & Chelsea*) • Ian *WRIGHT* (*Arsenal & West Ham United*)
Peter *BEARDSLEY* (*Everton, Newcastle & Bolton*),

*Manager*
Sir Bobby *ROBSON* CBE

### *Did You Know That?*
Up to the end of May 2008, Gary Neville had made 85 appearances for England and scored just one goal, an own goal against Croatia.

## ❧ KEANE CENTURION ❧

Robbie Keane's goal for Tottenham Hotspur in their 2–0 Premiership win over Sunderland at White Hart Lane on 19 January 2008 was the Irish international striker's 100th for the club.

## ❧ AN IMPRESSIVE DEBUT ❧

Newcastle United, playing in their first season in the Premiership in 1993–94, finished third in the table behind champions Manchester United and runners-up Blackburn Rovers. The Magpies were spearheaded by their 22-year-old striker Andy Cole, who finished the season as the league's top scorer with 34 goals from 40 games.

## ❧ DAYS TO FORGET ❧

The following table lists the all-time record margins of defeat suffered by the 2007–08 Premier League clubs:

| Team | Opponents | Score | Year |
|---|---|---|---|
| Reading | Preston North End | 18–0 | 1894 |
| Fulham | Liverpool | 10–0 | 1986 |
| Portsmouth | Leicester City | 10–0 | 1928 |
| Derby County | Everton | 11–2 | 1889 |
| Middlesbrough | Blackburn Rovers | 9–0 | 1954 |
| Newcastle United | Burton | 9–0 | 1895 |
| Birmingham City | Sheffield Wednesday | 9–1 | 1930 |
| Bolton Wanderers | Preston North End | 9–1 | 1887 |
| Liverpool | Birmingham City | 9–1 | 1954 |
| Manchester City | Everton | 9–1 | 1906 |
| Arsenal | Loughborough | 8–0 | 1896 |
| Blackburn Rovers | Arsenal | 8–0 | 1933 |
| Sunderland | Sheffield Wednesday | 8–0 | 1911 |
| Tottenham Hotspur | IFC Cologne | 8–0 | 1995 |
| Aston Villa | Blackburn Rovers | 8–1 | 1889 |
| Chelsea | Wolves | 8–1 | 1953 |
| Manchester United | Blackburn Rovers | 7–0 | 1926 |
| West Ham United | Blackburn Rovers | 8–2 | 1963 |
| Everton | Tottenham Hotspur | 10–4 | 1958 |
| Wigan Athletic | Bristol Rovers | 6–1 | 1990 |

## ❧ A NEW VILLAIN IN TOWN ❧

In February 1998, Brian Little left the managerial hot seat at Aston Villa and was replaced by Wycombe Wanderers' John Gregory. Gregory had previously been a coach at Villa Park, and after taking charge he guided the team to seventh place in the Premiership and automatic UEFA Cup qualification.

## ❧ THE TEESIDE HERO ❧

When Middlesbrough won the League Cup in 2003–04, Steve McClaren became the first English manager to win one of English football's three major prizes since Brian Little guided Aston Villa to League Cup success over Leeds United in 1996. McClaren was also the first man to take Middlesbrough into European competition, as they qualified for the 2004–05 UEFA Cup.

## ALL CHANGE AT ANFIELD

After enjoying a good World Cup in the summer of 2002, Senegal player El Hadji Diouf was signed for Liverpool by manager Gerard Houllier. The arrival of the Senegalese international at Anfield signalled the end of Nicolas Anelka's loan stay at the club and he was sold to newly promoted Manchester City by his Turkish club Trabzonspor for £13 million. However, this was far from the end of the Reds' summer transfer dealings as Houllier then handed over £4.5 million for the French international winger Bruno Cheyrou, while Nick Barmby, Jari Litmanen and the long-serving Jamie Redknapp followed Anelka out of Anfield.

## HUNG-UP OVER YOU

At the end of the 2005–06 season two of the Premiership's outstanding players, Dennis Bergkamp of Arsenal and Newcastle United's Alan Shearer, hung up their football boots for good. Shearer had hoped to play until the end of the campaign, but minutes after converting a penalty to give the Toon Army the lead against Sunderland at the Stadium of Light on 17 April 2006, he suffered a knee injury that brought his career to a premature close.

## NO CHARITY FOR THE GEORDIES

On 11 August 1996, Manchester United faced Newcastle United in the traditional opener to the new football season, the FA Charity Shield at Wembley. Manchester United won the game 4–0.

## STRIKER GOES ON STRIKE

Nottingham Forest's Pierre van Hooijdonk went on strike at the start of the 1998–99 season. Forest's leading goalscorer when they won the First Division championship the previous season was unhappy with the news that fellow strike-partner Kevin Campbell had been sold to Trabzonspor in Turkey for £2.5 million. During the 1997–98 season van Hooijdonk scored 34 times for Forest and Campbell found the net 24 times. The Dutch striker asked for a transfer, but it was refused, so he kept fit by training with one of his former clubs, NAC Breda in the Netherlands. He eventually returned to the City Ground in October 1998, but by then Forest where already in a relegation battle, sitting bottom of the Premiership without a win in nine league games, and eventually failed to beat the drop.

## ❧ TOOTHLESS UP FRONT ❧

Manchester City finished 16th in the Premiership table during the 1993–94 season and scored a miserable 38 goals, with their leading league goalscorer only finding the back of the net six times. It was their lowest finish in the top flight since suffering relegation from Division One at the end of the 1986–87 season. City were so poor up front that all three relegated clubs scored more goals than them, while only Ipswich Town scored fewer, with 35.

## ❧ BORING, BORING ARSENAL ❧

Although a total of 1,222 goals were scored in the inaugural FA Premier League season of 1992–93, Arsenal only accounted for 40 of them, the lowest goals tally of any of the 22 teams in the League. The Gunners, First Division champions in 1991, finished in tenth place.

## ❧ THE HAT-TRICK KING ❧

Alan Shearer has scored more hat-tricks in the Premier League than any other player in its 16-year history (1992–2008). Here is the top five:

| Player | Clubs | No. of hat-tricks |
|---|---|---|
| 1. Alan Shearer | Blackburn, Newcastle | 11 |
| 2. Robbie Fowler | Leeds, Liverpool | 9 |
| 3. Thierry Henry | Arsenal | 8 |
| =3. Michael Owen | Liverpool, Newcastle | 8 |
| =5. Andy Cole | Newcastle, Manchester Utd | 5 |
| =5. Ian Wright | Arsenal | 5 |

## ❧ MACCA AND GROWLER PARTNERSHIP ❧

Robbie Fowler and Steve McManaman have a horseracing business – "The Macca and Growler Partnership". They have several horses with trainer Martin Pipe.

## ❧ KENNY'S RUUD REPLACEMENT ❧

Shortly after the start of the 1998–99 Premiership season Newcastle United sacked manager Kenny Dalglish and replaced him with the former Chelsea player-coach Ruud Gullit.

## ❧ OLD GUNS MAKE WAY FOR NEW GUNS ❧

After helping Arsenal to the domestic Double in season 2001–02, Tony Adams, aged 35, and Lee Dixon, aged 38, retired. Adams had been at the club for 19 years, 14 of them as captain, while Dixon had been there for 14 years. Shortly after starting a Sports Science degree at Brunel University, Adams was appointed the manager of Wycombe Wanderers in November 2003, but he could not save them from relegation to League Two in season 2003–04. He resigned in November 2004 and, in July 2005, he took up a trainee coaching post with the Dutch side Feyenoord before moving to Portsmouth in June 2006 as assistant to manager Harry Redknapp. Following the departure of Adams, Arsene Wenger appointed Patrick Vieira as the new Arsenal captain for the 2002–03 season.

## ❧ PROLIFIC AL ❧

In season 1995–96 Blackburn Rovers, the defending Premiership Champions, could only manage a seventh-place finish in the Premiership table. Rovers scored 61 Premier League goals from their 38 games, and remarkably Alan Shearer scored 31 of them.

## ❧ INTERWOVEN FATES ❧

In November 2002 Sunderland sacked their manager Peter Reid and replaced him at the Stadium of Light with Howard Wilkinson. In March 2003 Reid was appointed the interim manager of Leeds United after they sacked Terry Venables – Wilkinson having been the manager of Leeds United from 1988 to 1996. Moreover, Venables was England manager from 1994 to 1996, and later Wilkinson managed the England team on a caretaker capacity in 1999 after Glenn Hoddle was sacked.

## ❧ PLAYING BY NUMBERS ❧

The following table lists the top-five players with the highest shirt number to appear in the 2007–08 Premier League season:

|   |   |   |   |
|---|---|---|---|
| 1. | Gizegroz Rasiak | Bolton Wanderers | No.47 |
| 2. | Rade Prica | Sunderland | No.45 |
| =3. | Jonny Evans | Sunderland | No.44 |
| =3. | Chris Gunter | Tottenham Hotspur | No.44 |
| =3. | Robbie Savage | Derby County | No.44 |

# ✌ ROY KEANE ✍

"Fail to prepare, prepare to fail" is a line from Roy's autobiography, simply entitled *Keane*, and this just about summed up Roy's playing career. Roy was a warrior on the pitch, who would lead from the front as he took the battle to the opposition. Outspoken by nature, he was a powerful, aggressive player who never shirked a tackle and a true midfield general, who was the driving force of Manchester United's midfield for 12 years from 1993 to 2005.

Roy Maurice Keane was born in Cork, Republic of Ireland, on 10 August 1971. In 1989 he signed as a semi-professional with Cobh Ramblers before joining Brian Clough's Nottingham Forest for £20,000. Few players can say that they played for two managerial legends, but Keano can. After Forest were relegated at the end of the 1993 season, Roy received overtures from a number of clubs. He chose Manchester United, the inaugural FA Premier League winners, and joined for a record transfer fee of £3.75 million. In his first season at Old Trafford, United won the Double, a feat they repeated in season 1995–96.

After United had clinched their fourth Premiership crown in five seasons in 1996–97, Keano was appointed the captain following the shock retirement of Eric Cantona. United's inspirational captain missed much of the 1997–98 season with a cruciate knee-ligament injury, but returned for the 1998–99 season and helped guide the side to the unprecedented Treble, although he missed the dramatic Champions League final win over Bayern Munich through suspension. In 2000 Keano was voted the PFA Players' Player of the Year.

Roy captained Manchester United to nine major honours, making him the Red Devils' most successful captain of all time. During his time at Old Trafford, United won seven league titles, four FA Cups, the UEFA Champions League and the Intercontinental Cup. In January 2006 Keano left United and joined Celtic, where he won the Scottish Premier League and Scottish League Cup, before hanging up his boots in May 2006.

In August 2006, the lure of management took him to Sunderland's Stadium of Light where he was reunited with his former international team-mate Niall Quinn, the club's chairman. In his first season as a manager he guided the Black Cats to the Championship title and promotion back to the Premier League.

### Did You Know That?

At international level, Keano played for Ireland 66 times, but missed out on the 2002 World Cup finals in Japan and South Korea after a pre-tournament spat with team manager Mick McCarthy.

## ℜ PREMIERSHIP TALK (12) ℘

"You see how Spanish, Italians, Portuguese play football. I don't say they are perfect, I say English football has a few things to learn from them in the same way they have a lot of things to learn from English football."
*Chelsea manager Jose Mourinho*

## ℜ KEANE MEMBER OF ELITE CENTURIONS ℘

When Robbie Keane scored for Spurs against Sunderland on 19 January 2008, he became the 13th player to bag 100 or more Premier League goals. Of the other 12 centurions, only Andy Cole, Michael Owen and Dwight Yorke appeared in the Premiership in 2007–08. Here are the elite marksmen, together with the total number of Premiership goals to their name up to the day on which the Irish international striker Keane joined their select group:

❖ 261 – Alan Shearer (retired) ❖
❖ 187 – Andy Cole (at Sunderland – but on loan at Burnley) ❖
❖ 171 – Thierry Henry (at FC Barcelona) ❖
❖ 161 – Robbie Fowler (at Cardiff City) ❖
❖ 150 – Les Ferdinand (retired) ❖
❖ 147 – Teddy Sheringham (at Colchester United) ❖
❖ 128 – Jimmy-Floyd Hasselbaink (at Cardiff City) ❖
❖ 127 – Michael Owen (at Newcastle United) ❖
❖ 127 – Dwight Yorke (at Sunderland) ❖
❖ 113 – Ian Wright (retired) ❖
❖ 111 – Dion Dublin (at Norwich City) ❖
❖ 100 – Matthew Le Tissier (retired) ❖
❖ 100 – Robbie Keane (at Tottenham Hotspur) ❖

## ℜ GEORDIES' RECORD START ℘

In 1994–95 Newcastle United made the best start in the top flight in the club's history, winning their first six games to go top of the Premiership. However, they ended the season in sixth place.

## ℜ SAINTS MOVE TO ST MARY'S ℘

The 2000–01 season was Southampton's last season at The Dell and after 103 years the Saints moved to their new all-seater stadium at St Mary's. With a 32,000 capacity, St Mary's contained more than twice the number of seats than The Dell.

## ❧ FINAL PREMIERSHIP TABLE 2000–2001 ❦

| Pos | Team | P | W | D | L | F | A | Pts |
|---|---|---|---|---|---|---|---|---|
| 1. | Manchester United (C) | 38 | 24 | 8 | 6 | 79 | 31 | 80 |
| 2. | Arsenal | 38 | 20 | 10 | 8 | 63 | 38 | 70 |
| 3. | Liverpool | 38 | 20 | 9 | 9 | 71 | 39 | 69 |
| 4. | Leeds United | 38 | 20 | 8 | 10 | 64 | 43 | 68 |
| 5. | Ipswich Town | 38 | 20 | 6 | 12 | 57 | 42 | 66 |
| 6. | Chelsea | 38 | 17 | 10 | 11 | 68 | 45 | 61 |
| 7. | Sunderland | 38 | 15 | 12 | 11 | 46 | 41 | 57 |
| 8. | Aston Villa | 38 | 13 | 15 | 10 | 46 | 43 | 54 |
| 9. | Charlton Athletic | 38 | 14 | 10 | 14 | 50 | 57 | 52 |
| 10. | Southampton | 38 | 14 | 10 | 14 | 40 | 48 | 52 |
| 11. | Newcastle United | 38 | 14 | 9 | 15 | 44 | 50 | 51 |
| 12. | Tottenham Hotspur | 38 | 13 | 10 | 15 | 47 | 54 | 49 |
| 13. | Leicester City | 38 | 14 | 6 | 18 | 39 | 51 | 48 |
| 14. | Middlesbrough | 38 | 9 | 15 | 14 | 44 | 44 | 42 |
| 15. | West Ham United | 38 | 10 | 12 | 16 | 45 | 50 | 42 |
| 16. | Everton | 38 | 11 | 9 | 18 | 45 | 59 | 42 |
| 17. | Derby County | 38 | 10 | 12 | 16 | 37 | 59 | 42 |
| 18. | Manchester City (R) | 38 | 8 | 10 | 20 | 41 | 65 | 34 |
| 19. | Coventry City (R) | 38 | 8 | 10 | 20 | 36 | 63 | 34 |
| 20. | Bradford City (R) | 38 | 5 | 11 | 22 | 30 | 70 | 26 |

## ❧ FERGIE THE PEACEMAKER ❦

On 15th February 2008, Eamonn Holmes had Prime Minister Gordon Brown as a guest on his BBC Radio 5 show. Mr Brown confessed to being a Raith Rovers fan but said he also liked Tottenham Hotspur and Manchester United. Indeed, the PM went as far as to suggest that Sir Alex Ferguson could help to bring peace to the Middle East: "Prime Minister Olmert of Israel and Mr Fayyad, Prime Minister of the Palestinian Authority, are both United supporters. We had a plan at one stage that I would take them both to a match. I have found, to my great surprise, that sport is actually a means by which people work and communicate," said Mr Brown.

## ❧ MOVING SOUTH ❦

On 27 November 2007, Alex McLeish resigned as manager of Scotland's national side. The following day he was unveiled by Birmingham City as Steve Bruce's successor. Bruce had quit the Blues on 19 November 2007 to take charge of Wigan Athletic.

## ⚜ THE HOT SEATS ⚜

Of all the clubs that have played in the Premiership since its inaugural season in 1992–93, only Manchester United have not changed their manager. Sir Alex Ferguson has been in charge of the Red Devils since November 1986. Of the 20 Premiership clubs in 2007–08, the following have seen the most managerial changes since 1992:

1. Wigan Athletic................................11 managers
=2. Portsmouth.................................10 managers
=2. Tottenham Hotspur.....................10 managers
=4. Fulham............................................9 managers
=4. Manchester City...........................9 managers

*Did You Know That?*
Arsenal have had just three different managers in the Premiership: George Graham, Bruce Rioch and Arsene Wenger. Stewart Houston and Pat Rice both filled in as caretaker managers during this time.

## ⚜ AN UNHAPPY ENDING ⚜

In their final home game of the 2002–03 season Manchester City lost to Southampton in the Premier League. It was the Citizens' last ever game at Maine Road before moving to Eastlands (aka the City of Manchester Stadium, venue for the 2002 Commonwealth Games).

## ⚜ THE KOP'S LAST STAND ⚜

"The Kop's Last Stand" was the name given to Liverpool's match programme for the visit of Norwich City to Anfield on 30 April 1994 in the Premiership. It marked the last-ever game in front of a standing Kop, and before the match a tearful Gerry Marsden performed the Liverpool anthem "You'll Never Walk Alone". However, many Liverpool fans among the crowd of 44,339 will want to forget the game itself since Norwich City spoiled the party, winning 1–0 thanks to a goal from Jeremy Goss – in front of the Kop!

## ⚜ WHEN THE WELL WENT DRY ⚜

When Manchester City lost their final home 1–0 to Manchester United on 5 May 2007, they set a new record for the fewest goals scored at home in a season by a club in the top flight, a meagre ten. City had not scored at home since New Year's Day 2007.

## ✨ THE COSTLY LADS ✨

There have been many sizeable transfers since the inaugural Premier League in season 1992–93. The following table lists the all-time Top 11 highest transfer fees received by a Premiership club after the January 2008 transfer window closed:

1. Rio Ferdinand ............... Leeds United to Manchester United .... £29.1m
2. David Beckham ............... Manchester United to Real Madrid ......... £25m
3. Nicolas Anelka ............... Arsenal to Real Madrid ........................... £23m
4. Shaun Wright-Phillips ... Manchester City to Chelsea ...................... £21m
5. Wayne Rooney ............... Everton to Manchester United ................. £20m
6. Michael Carrick ............... Spurs to Manchester United ................. £18.6m
7. Rio Ferdinand ............... West Ham to Leeds United ...................... £18m
8. Damien Duff ............... Blackburn Rovers to Chelsea ................... £17m
9. Nicolas Anelka ............... Bolton Wanderers to Chelsea ................. £15m
10. Alan Shearer ............... Blackburn Rovers to Newcastle United .... £15m

## ✨ PREMIER LEAGUE'S EUROPEAN TRIO ✨

At the end of the 1998–99 season UEFA increased the Premiership's UEFA Champions League places for the 1999–2000 season to three. Manchester United qualified as Premiership champions and Arsenal as runners-up, while Chelsea grabbed the final qualifying place by coming third. Meanwhile fourth-placed Leeds United qualified for the UEFA Cup, and fifth-placed West Ham United also gained a UEFA Cup place via the Intertoto Cup route. Tottenham Hotspur, League Cup winners, and Newcastle United, FA Cup runners-up, also claimed UEFA Cup slots.

## ✨ THREE BOSSES, ONE RELEGATION ✨

In October 2001 Jim Smith rejected Derby County's offer of a position as director of football and resigned as manager. Smith was replaced as manager by Colin Todd, who had won First Division championship-winners' medals as a player with Derby County in 1972 and 1975. However, Todd only lasted 18 games in charge before being sacked following an embarrassing FA Cup third-round exit to Division Three side Bristol Rovers. He was replaced by John Gregory, who had been sacked as manager of Aston Villa less than a week earlier. However, the Rams ended the season one place off the foot of the Premiership table and were relegated to Division One.

## ❧ TIGHT GUNNERS ❧

Despite conceding 20 fewer Premiership goals (17 to 37) than Manchester United in the 1998–99 season, Arsenal were still pipped to the Premier League title thanks to United's awesome firepower. With their strike force of Andy Cole, Teddy Sheringham, Ole Gunnar Solskjaer and Dwight Yorke, United scored 21 more Premiership goals than their title challengers (80 to 59).

## ❧ OFF WITHOUT A TOUCH ❧

Andreas Johansson and Keith Gillespie are joint holders of the unenviable Premiership record for the fewest touches of a ball in a game before being sent off. On 7 May 2006, Johansson came on as a substitute for Wigan Athletic against Arsenal and was quickly sent off, and Gillespie came on as a substitute for Sheffield United against Reading on 20 January 2007 and was also sent for a very early bath. Neither player touched the ball.

## ❧ WHO ATE ALL THE PIES? ❧

On the opening day of the 1993–94 season Coventry City visited Arsenal, the reigning FA Cup and League Cup holders, and came away with a 3–0 win courtesy of a hat-trick from Micky Quinn. During his two years with Coventry City (1992–94), Micky Quinn was nicknamed "Sumo" and was once famously hailed as the Premiership's "fastest player over a yard". In 2003, Quinn released his autobiography entitled *Who Ate All the Pies?*

## ❧ UNITED – A CLOSED BOOK ❧

By Christmas 2000 Manchester United were so far ahead of the chasing pack in the Premiership that the bookmakers closed their books on anyone catching them. United streaked to the title ten points clear of the Gunners and 11 in front of third-placed Liverpool.

## ❧ DEAD-EYE DARREN ❧

At the end of the 2007–08 season, Darren Anderton, the former Tottenham Hotspur and Birmingham City player, was the all-time leading dead-ball specialist in the history of the Premiership, with 56 goals resulting from one of his corners or free-kicks.

## ⚜ PREMIERSHIP TALK (13) ⚜

"I may be French, but I'm playing for Arsenal."
**Thierry Henry** *(Arsenal)*

## ⚜ PREMIER LEAGUE READING STARS ⚜

As part of the Premier League Reading Stars programme, players were asked to nominate a favourite book. Here is a selection of the responses:

❖ *The Day of the Jackal* by Frederick Forsythe (Dirk Kuyt) ❖
❖ *Why is Snot Green?* by Glenn Murphy (David James) ❖
❖ *The Damned United* by David Peace (Jermaine Jenas) ❖
❖ *Of Mice and Men* by John Steinbeck (Matthew Upson) ❖
❖ *James and the Giant Peach* by Roald Dahl (Michael Ball) ❖
❖ *Charlie and the Chocolate Factory* by Roald Dahl (Scott Carson) ❖
❖ *Sacred Stone* by Clive Cussler (Marcus Hahnemann) ❖

## ⚜ MERSEYSIDE ESCAPOLOGISTS ⚜

Everton only managed to avoid the drop into Division One at the end of the 1997–98 Premiership season on the final day on goal difference at the expense of Bolton Wanderers.

## ⚜ A GREAT ESCAPE IN LONDON ⚜

Following a number of defeats in January and February 2003, Leeds United were deep in a Premiership relegation battle. Having sacked David O'Leary the previous summer, the Leeds board then sacked his successor Terry Venables and replaced him with ex-Sunderland manager Peter Reid. In their penultimate game of the season, Leeds faced a daunting trip to London to play the reigning Premiership champions, Arsenal, themselves involved in a tense battle for the title with Manchester United. Remarkably, Leeds beat Arsenal 3–2 at Highbury, a result that ensured their Premiership survival – the result also handed Manchester United the Premiership crown.

## ⚜ DOUBLE ROBBIE ⚜

At the end of the 1995–96 season Liverpool's Robbie Fowler won the PFA Young Player of the Year award for the second year in succession. In January 1996 he also became the first player to win the Premier League Player of the Month Award in successive months.

## ☒ HEY, BIG SPENDERS ☒

When Fulham signed Danny Murphy from Spurs on the last day of the transfer window, 31 August 2007, they set a new Premier League record for the highest number of summer signings, 15.

## ☒ A DOUBLE LEGEND SWOOP ☒

At the end of the 1994–95 season, Glenn Hoddle, Chelsea's player-manager, hung up his football boots for good to concentrate on managing the Blues. Amazingly, Hoddle managed to persuade Manchester United's Mark Hughes and AC Milan's Ruud Gullit to join his Stamford Bridge revolution.

## ☒ EX-MEMBERS' UNIQUE TREBLE ☒

Charlton Athletic made a return to the Premiership tt the end of the 1999–2000 season by winning the First Division title. Manchester City finished runners-up to Charlton and were also promoted along with Ipswich Town, the First Division play-off winners. It was the first time in the eight-year history of the Premier League that the three teams promoted from the First Division were all former Premier League clubs.

## ☒ UNFIT FOR PREMIER LEAGUE SURVIVAL ☒

Middlesbrough had a rollercoaster season in 1996–97. They lost both domestic cup finals and were relegated from the Premiership in 19th place. However, Boro would have escaped relegation if they had not been docked three points by the Premier League as a punishment for postponing a league game against Blackburn Rovers in January 1997, just 24 hours before the game. The FA's assistant chief executive originally gave Boro permission to postpone the game, only for the FA to decide that the game should proceed after all. If Boro had played the game and replaced their first-team players with reserves and youth teamers they would have stayed up. The three points they lost would have secured 16th place in the Premiership and sent Coventry City down. Indeed, if they had won the game when it was played in May 1997 – they drew 0–0 – they would have survived. Boro's chairman Steve Gibson lodged an appeal with the Premier League at the time of the points deduction, claiming that the club simply did not have enough fit players to field a team, but the appeal was unsuccessful.

## ❧ BRITISH FOOTBALL'S RICH LIST ❧

In November 2007 the football magazine *Four Four Two* published lists of the ten wealthiest men in British football and the ten richest players in British football (including England internationals not playing in the English leagues):

### Top-Ten Richest Men in British Football

| | | | |
|---|---|---|---|
| 1. | Roman Abramovich | Chelsea | £10.8bn |
| 2. | Joe Lewis | Tottenham Hotspur | £2.8bn |
| 3. | Alisher Usmanov | Arsenal | £2.7bn |
| 4. | Bernie Ecclestone | Queen's Park Rangers | £2.5bn |
| =5. | Mike Ashley | Newcastle United | £1.6bn |
| =5. | Dermot Desmond | Glasgow Celtic | £1.6bn |
| 7. | Malcolm Glazer | Manchester United | £1.25bn |
| 8. | Stanley Kroenke | Arsenal | £1.2bn |
| 9. | Trevor Hemmings | Preston North End | £980m |
| 10. | Lord Ashcroft | Watford | £950m |

### Top-Ten Richest British Footballers

| | | | |
|---|---|---|---|
| 1. | David Beckham | LA Galaxy | £112m |
| 2. | Michael Owen | Newcastle United | £37m |
| =3. | Robbie Fowler | Cardiff City | £30m |
| =3. | Wayne Rooney | Manchester United | £30m |
| 5. | Sol Campbell | Portsmouth | £28m |
| =6. | Andrei Shevchenko | Chelsea | £25m |
| =6. | Rio Ferdinand | Manchester United | £25m |
| 8. | Ryan Giggs | Manchester United | £23m |
| 9. | Michael Ballack | Chelsea | £18m |
| 10. | Steven Gerrard | Liverpool | £15m |

## ❧ 15,000 VOLZ ❧

On 30 December 2006, Moritz Volz of Fulham scored the 15,000th FA Premier League goal in his side's 2–2 draw away to Chelsea. Barclaycard, the FA Premier League's sponsor, donated £15,000 to the Fulham Community Sports Trust in Volz's name. Meanwhile, a fan who correctly predicted that the German would score the historic goal, in a contest organized by the Premier League, was afforded the honour of presenting the player with a special award prior to Fulham's home game versus Watford at Craven Cottage on New Year's Day 2007. Since netting the historic strike, the Fulham fans have given the German the nickname "15,000 Volz".

## ⚜ THE SHERIFF OF NOTTINGHAM ⚜

In October 1998, Nottingham Forest sacked manager Dave Bassett and replaced him with Ron Atkinson until the end of the 1998–99 season. In Big Ron's first game in charge of Forest, a home game against Arsenal, he famously walked into the opposition's dugout and sat down. When asked about it after the match, he waved the incident off in true Big Ron fashion. "For a moment I thought we had Bergkamp on our bench," said the new Forest boss. Unfortunately Atkinson could not save Forest from the drop into Division One at the end of the 1998–99 season, when they finished bottom of the table. In his 16 games in charge at the City Ground Big Ron won four, drew two and lost ten. After Forest's relegation Atkinson retired and David Platt, the former England captain, was brought to the club as player-manager.

## ⚜ MILLENNIUM TOPPERS ⚜

On New Year's Day 2000 Leeds United entered the new millennium sitting on top of the Premiership table. However, David O'Leary's side eventually finished the 1999–2000 season in third place – a yawning 22 points behind the runaway champions Manchester United.

## ⚜ THE DYNAMIC DUO ⚜

Andy Cole (34 goals) and Peter Beardsley (25 goals) scored 59 goals for Newcastle United in their 1993–94 Premiership campaign and both made the top three of the goalscoring charts for the season. The rest of the team only managed 23 between them while the Geordies, managed by their former player Kevin Keegan in their first season back in the top flight, finished third in the table and qualified for the UEFA Cup. Not surprisingly, Andy Cole won the 1993–94 PFA Young Player of the Year Award.

## ⚜ FROM DUGOUT TO DESK JOB ⚜

On 28 January 2008, Dennis Wise resigned as manager of Leeds United to take up his new role as director of football development at Newcastle United. Fans at both clubs were left stunned by Wise's move, which came less than a fortnight after Kevin Keegan had made a hero's return to St James' Park, succeeding Sam Allardyce as boss of the Magpies. Wise left with Leeds sitting in fifth place in League One, despite the club starting the season with a 15-point deduction.

# ✂ HISPANIC PREMIER LEAGUE FANTASY XI ✂

**1**
Jose Manuel
*REINA*
*(SPAIN)*

**2**
Albert
*FERRER*
*(SPAIN, capt.)*

**4**
Ricardo
*CARVALHO*
*(PORTUGAL)*

**5**
Gabriel
*HEINZE*
*(ARGENTINA)*

**3**
Paulo
*FERREIRA*
*(PORTUGAL)*

**7**
Cristiano
*RONALDO*
*(PORTUGAL)*

**6**
Javier
*MASCHERANO*
*(ARGENTINA)*

**8**
Cesc
*FABREGAS*
*(SPAIN)*

**9**
Fernando
*TORRES*
*(SPAIN)*

**10**
Carlos
*TEVEZ*
*(ARGENTINA)*

**11**
*JUNINHO*
*(BRAZIL)*

*Substitutes*
Manuel *ALMUNIA (Spain)* • Juliano *BELETTI (Brazil)* • Gilberto *SILVA (Brazil)*
Roque *SANTA CRUZ (Paraguay)* • Juan Sebastian *VERON (Argentina)*
*Manager*
Jose *MOURINHO (Portugal)*

### *Did You Know That?*

Juliano Beletti scored the winning goal in the 2006 UEFA
Champions League final for Barcelona against Arsenal.

## ✂ LANDLORDS RELEGATED ✂

In the inaugural Premiership season in 1992–93, Crystal Palace
and Wimbledon both played their home games at Selhurst Park,
London. At the end of the season Palace were relegated while the
Dons, who rented the ground, finished a respectable 12th in the
Premier League table.

## ✂ POPE SUPPORTS LIVERPOOL ✂

In 2004 Pope John Paul II granted an audience with players from the
Polish national football team. During the audience in the Vatican, the
Pontiff – who was born in Poland and was a goalkeeper in his youth
– told Liverpool No.1 Jerzy Dudek that he was a keen supporter of the
Reds and listened out for their results whenever they were playing.

## ❧ TOP WINS FOR RELEGATED SIDES ❧

Barnsley top a table of clubs with the most wins by a relegated club in a 38-game Premier League season with ten. They share this dubious honour with four other clubs.

| | | |
|---|---|---|
| =1. | Barnsley | 1997–98 |
| =1. | Sheffield United | 2006–07 |
| =1. | Sunderland | 1996–97 |
| =1. | West Ham United | 2002–03 |
| =1. | Reading | 2007–08 |

## ❧ ROVERS SKIPPING AGAIN ❧

In season 1997–98 Roy Hodgson guided Blackburn Rovers to sixth place in the Premiership and UEFA Cup football the following season. Chris Sutton ended the season as the Premiership's joint top goalscorer (18 goals) which was good enough to earn him a call-up to the England team. Sutton played in England's 2–0 friendly win over Cameroon at Wembley on 15 November 1997, his first and last cap for his country.

## ❧ SPARKY OF THE ROVERS ❧

In season 2001–02 Blackburn Rovers lay third from bottom of the Premiership table when they faced Tottenham Hotspur in the Worthington (League) Cup final at the Millennium Stadium in Cardiff. However, the 1995 Premiership champions beat Spurs 2–1 to win the cup, and a good run of form then enabled Graeme Souness' side to climb away from the relegation zone and end the campaign tenth in the table.

This winners medal was the last one won by striker Mark Hughes, who retired at the end of the 2001–02 season. Hughes, nicknamed Sparky, had an illustrious career that saw him capped 72 times by Wales, as well as playing for Manchester United (two spells), Barcelona, Bayern Munich (on loan), Chelsea, Southampton and Everton. With United, Sparky won three FA Cups (1985, 1990 and 1994), two Premier League titles (1993 and 1994), the League Cup (1992), the European Cup Winners' Cup (1991) and the European Super Cup (1991). During his time at Chelsea he added to his medal collection with a fourth FA Cup (1997), a second League Cup (1998) and a second European Cup Winners' Cup (1998).

# ❧ FINAL PREMIERSHIP TABLE 2001–2002 ❧

| Pos | Team | P | W | D | L | F | A | Pts |
|---|---|---|---|---|---|---|---|---|
| 1. | Arsenal (C) | 38 | 26 | 9 | 3 | 79 | 36 | 87 |
| 2. | Liverpool | 38 | 24 | 8 | 6 | 67 | 30 | 80 |
| 3. | Manchester United | 38 | 24 | 5 | 9 | 87 | 45 | 77 |
| 4. | Newcastle United | 38 | 21 | 8 | 9 | 74 | 52 | 71 |
| 5. | Leeds United | 38 | 18 | 12 | 8 | 53 | 37 | 66 |
| 6. | Chelsea | 38 | 17 | 13 | 8 | 66 | 38 | 64 |
| 7. | West Ham United | 38 | 15 | 8 | 15 | 48 | 57 | 53 |
| 8. | Aston Villa | 38 | 12 | 14 | 12 | 46 | 47 | 50 |
| 9. | Tottenham Hotspur | 38 | 14 | 8 | 16 | 49 | 53 | 50 |
| 10. | Blackburn Rovers | 38 | 12 | 10 | 16 | 55 | 51 | 46 |
| 11. | Southampton | 38 | 12 | 9 | 17 | 46 | 54 | 45 |
| 12. | Middlesbrough | 38 | 12 | 9 | 17 | 35 | 47 | 45 |
| 13. | Fulham | 38 | 10 | 14 | 14 | 36 | 44 | 44 |
| 14. | Charlton Athletic | 38 | 10 | 14 | 14 | 38 | 49 | 44 |
| 15. | Everton | 38 | 11 | 10 | 17 | 45 | 57 | 43 |
| 16. | Bolton Wanderers | 38 | 9 | 13 | 16 | 44 | 62 | 40 |
| 17. | Sunderland | 38 | 10 | 10 | 18 | 29 | 51 | 40 |
| 18. | Ipswich Town (R) | 38 | 9 | 9 | 20 | 41 | 64 | 36 |
| 19. | Derby County (R) | 38 | 8 | 6 | 24 | 33 | 63 | 30 |
| 20. | Leicester City (R) | 38 | 5 | 13 | 20 | 30 | 64 | 28 |

## ❧ ARSENAL, LONDON'S FIFTH BEST CLUB ❧

In 1994–95, Arsenal, First Division winners in 1988–89 and 1990–91, finished 12th in the Premiership, and fifth among London's seven clubs. Above Arsenal were: Chelsea (11th), Wimbledon (ninth), Queen's Park Rangers (eighth), and Tottenham Hotspur (seventh). West Ham United were (14th) and Crystal Palace (19th).

## ❧ QUAKING IN HIS BOOTS ❧

Faustino Asprilla, who joined Newcastle United during the 1995–96 season, was the first Colombian footballer to be sent off in an international when he assaulted Paraguay's legendary goalkeeper Jose Luis Felix Chilavert during a World Cup qualifying match in 1997. Asprilla scored 20 goals in 57 matches for his country and infamously almost signed for Darlington in the English League Division Two as a favour to their chairman, with whom he was very good friends. However, when the day came for him to put pen to paper for the Quakers, Asprilla did a runner and fled the country.

## ❧ PREMIERSHIP TALK (14) ❧

"I prefer to play and lose rather than win, because I know in advance I'm going to win."
*Eric Cantona (Manchester United)*

## ❧ ELLAND ROAD MERRY-GO-ROUND ❧

In November 2003, Leeds United sacked their manager Peter Reid and appointed the club's first-team coach Eddie Gray as interim manager until the end of the 2003–04 season. When Gray, a Leeds United star of the 1970s, failed to save the Yorkshire club from relegation to the Championship, he was also sacked and replaced by his assistant Kevin Blackwell.

## ❧ BACK-TO-BACK DOUBLE FOR UNITED ❧

In season 1996–97, Manchester United won their second consecutive Premiership title and their fourth Championship in five seasons. It was also the second time the Red Devils achieved back-to-back Premier League titles, having previously won a second successive title in 1993–94. It was far from plain sailing, however – in October they lost three games and conceded 13 goals.

## ❧ FIRST OF THE MILLENNIUM ❧

The 1999–2000 season was the eighth of the Premier League, which was won by Manchester United, the reigning champions from 1998–99, as they claimed their sixth Premiership crown. Whereas the previous season Arsenal took the contest for the title right down to the wire – the Red Devils eventually pipped the Gunners by a single point – this time United romped away with the title, streets ahead of the opposition, winning the crown by a mammoth 18 points.

## ❧ THE NEW FACES ❧

Newcastle United (1993 Division One champions), West Ham United (1993 Division One runners-up) and Swindon Town (1993 Division One play-off final winners) all embarked on their first Premiership campaigns in season 1993–94. Only Swindon Town had never played in English football's top flight before: the Robins won the old Second Division play-off final in 1990, but were not allowed to take up their place in Division One because of financial irregularities.

## ❧ SPECIAL ONE DROPS BLUE BOMBSHELL ❧

Jose Mourinho sent shockwaves around the world of football when he left Chelsea by mutual consent on 20 September 2007, two days after their disappointing 1–1 home draw with Rosenborg in the UEFA Champions League and three days before their Premiership game against Manchester United at Old Trafford. The 44-year-old Portuguese manager arrived at Stamford Bridge in 2004 and won the Premier League title in his first two seasons in charge as well as the League Cup in 2005. In May 2007, he guided the Blues to FA Cup success and still had three years left on his contract, worth reputedly around £5 million a year. He took charge of Chelsea 185 times, winning 124 matches, drawing 40 and losing 21 – a record that also included a 60-match unbeaten home run in Premier League games.

## ❧ FOXES SIT ON TOP OF THE MOUNTAIN ❧

At the beginning of October 2000 Leicester City, under new manager Peter Taylor, sat proudly at the summit of the Premier League table. It was the first time since 1963 that Leicester City had reached such a dizzy height, and it only lasted two weeks, after which Manchester United assumed top spot and stayed there until the end of the season. Many Foxes fans thought that their club would struggle following Martin O'Neill's departure to manage Glasgow Celtic five months earlier, but Taylor ensured Premiership survival for Leicester City with a 13th-place finish in the table. However, it was the club's lowest finish since winning promotion to the Premiership in season 1995–96. In their last ten Premiership games of the season the Foxes suffered nine defeats and managed just one win. They never fully recovered from their shock home FA Cup exit to Second Division side Wycombe Wanderers.

## ❧ NOT SO SWEET SUGAR ❧

Tottenham Hotspur finished eighth at the end of the inaugural Premiership campaign in 1992–93, but chairman Alan Sugar sacked their chief executive, the highly popular Terry Venables, and his two head coaches Ray Clemence and Doug Livermore. Sugar helped curb the anger of the Spurs fans by appointing former hero Osvaldo Ardiles as the new man in charge at White Hart Lane. Ossie left West Bromwich Albion to take up the offer. Sugar's falling-out with Venables led to a High Court action, which Sugar won.

## ❧ LUCKY 13 FOR THE GEORDIES ❧

Despite only managing to finish in 13th place in the 1998–99 Premier
League season, Newcastle United qualified for the 1999–2000 UEFA
Cup competition because they lost in the final of the FA Cup (the
European Cup Winners' Cup was contested for the last time in 1998–
99). They lost to league champions Manchester United, who thus
completed the coveted domestic Double (and subsequent Treble).

## ❧ LONDON'S BIG SPENDERS ❧

Chelsea were able to spend heavily going into the 2003–04 season
thanks to their new owner Roman Abramovich's extensive bankroll.
Some £100 million was spent by Claudio Ranieri to strengthen his
side and push for the Premiership title. In the end, though, Chelsea
could only manage to finish runners-up to Arsenal.

## ❧ THOUSANDTH LIVE GAME ❧

The 1–1 draw between Tottenham Hotspur and Blackburn Rovers
at White Hart Lane on 10 May 2007 was the 1,000th live game to
be shown by Sky Sports.

## ❧ DIVER REPLACED ❧

During the summer of 1995, Tottenham Hotspur paid a club record
£4.5 million for Crystal Palace's Chris Armstrong to replace Jurgen
Klinsmann (labelled a "diver" prior to his arrival in England) who
had gone back to Germany. However, the 24-year old Armstrong
was labelled a "waste of money" by many Spurs fans, who considered
the fee to be too high for a player who had scored only nine goals for
the relegated Eagles and who had also failed a drugs test.

## ❧ THE DERBY KING ❧

Over the summer of 2001 Tottenham Hotspur purchased the German
international Christian Ziege from Liverpool. Ziege had only been
at Liverpool for a season and spent one season at Middlesbrough in
1999–2000. The stylish defender/midfielder began his career with
Bayern Munich (1990–97) before joining AC Milan (1997–99). He
is the only player to have played in the Munich, Milan, Tyne-Tees,
Merseyside and London derby matches. Ziege won the UEFA Cup
with Bayern Munich in 1996 and again with Liverpool in 2001.

# ⚜ JOSE MOURINHO ⚜

Jose Mario dos Santos Felix Mourinho was born in Setubal, Portugal, on 26 January 1963. His father, Felix, was a former goalkeeper and football manager. At college Mourinho obtained a degree in physical education, specializing in sports methodology. He joined Vila do Conde, where Felix was the head coach, and then completed a UEFA football coaching course. He then worked as a high school sports coach while trying unsuccessfully to make a career playing football.

After leaving his high school job he was given a backroom appointment at Estrela da Amadora before moving on to become a member of the coaching staff at Vitoria Setubal. Bobby Robson's arrival in Portugal in 1993 coincided with a turn in Mourinho's fortunes. When the former England manager was appointed manager of Sporting Lisbon in 1993 he hired Mourinho as his translator, and he took him with him when he moved to Porto in 1994. When Robson moved to Spain in 1996 to manage Barcelona, he again took Mourinho with him, but when Robson was fired in 1997, Mourinho stayed at the Nou Camp. Luis van Gaal, the new manager, actively involved Jose in team discussions and tactics before eventually allowing him to manage the Barcelona "B" team. In September 2000 his big chance came when he took up the manager's post at Benfica, but after being in charge for only nine league games they refused to grant him an extension to his contract and Jose resigned. He was appointed coach of Uniao de Leiria in January 2001 and guided them to their highest-ever league finish, fifth place, one place higher than Benfica. In January 2002, FC Porto installed Jose as their new manager and he quickly brought success to the club, winning two Portuguese championships (2003 and 2004), the Portuguese Cup (2003), the UEFA Cup (2003) and the UEFA Champions League (2004).

All of Europe now wanted Mourinho, but it was Chelsea, bankrolled by the Russian billionaire Roman Abramovich, who secured the services of the "Special One". When Jose walked through the gates of Stamford Bridge, Chelsea had not won the First Division title in 49 years, but he corrected that in his first season in charge (2004–05), having already won the Carling Cup three months earlier. Chelsea retained the Premiership title the following season and 2006–07 lifted both domestic Cups. On 20 September 2007, Mourinho sent shockwaves throughout the Premier League when he left Chelsea by "mutual consent".

### Did You Know That?
On 16 May 2007, Mourinho was arrested in London on suspicion of obstructing police following attempts to place his dog in quarantine.

## ❧ THE KING OF HAT-TRICK KINGS ❧

During the summer of 2004, West Bromwich Albion paid Cardiff City £3 million for the services of their Zambian-born Welsh international striker Robert Earnshaw. When Earnshaw scored a hat-trick for the Baggies in their Premiership win over Charlton Athletic on 19 March 2005, the Welsh striker became the first player to have bagged a hat-trick in all four levels of English professional league football (Premier League, Championship, League Divisions One and Two), in the FA Cup and League Cup and at international level.

## ❧ THE WHITE FEATHER ❧

Despite scoring 31 goals in all competitions for Middlesbrough, Fabrizio Ravanelli, nicknamed the "White Feather", could not save the club from relegation from the Premiership at the end of the 1996–97 season.

## ❧ MR BO JANGLES ❧

In February 1995, Coventry City sacked their manager Phil Neal and replaced him with Ron Atkinson, nicknamed "Big Ron" and "Mr Bo Jangles", who himself had been sacked by Aston Villa three months earlier. Atkinson moved quickly to bring in 37-year-old Gordon Strachan from Leeds United as his assistant manager, a move that paid off as the Sky Blues managed to avoid the drop, finishing 16th in the table.

## ❧ IN IT FOR THE LONG HAUL ❧

At the start of the 2007–08 season only three Premiership managers had been in charge of their respective clubs for five years or more:

| Manager | Club | Appointed |
|---|---|---|
| 1. Sir Alex Ferguson | Man Utd | 6 November 1986 |
| 2. Arsene Wenger | Arsenal | 30 September 1996 |
| 3. David Moyes | Everton | 15 March 2002 |

## ❧ THANKS FOR THE RELEGATION ❧

Following Watford's relegation from the FA Premier League at the end of the 2006–07 season, the club handed Andy Boothroyd a new three-year contract.

## ⚜ PREMIERSHIP TALK (15) ⚜

"I have shaved my head. My flowing locks are now quite a bit shorter."
**David Ginola** *(Aston Villa)*

## ⚜ FUTURE STARS ⚜

When Avram Grant guided Maccabi Haifa to their first Liga Leumit (Israeli Championship) success in seven years in the 2000–01 season, his young side contained future Premiership stars Yossi Benayoun and Aiyegbeni Yakubu.

## ⚜ THE MAGNIFICENT SEVEN RED DEVILS ⚜

In 1995–96 Manchester United became the first English side to repeat the domestic Double, and achieved the feat with seven players from their previous Double triumph in 1993–94.

## ⚜ EAGLES SWOOP BACK ⚜

Crystal Palace became the first team to be relegated from and promoted back to the Premier League when they won the Division One title in 1994. The Eagles were relegated at the end of the inaugural Premiership campaign in 1992–93 along with Middlesbrough and Nottingham Forest. However, Forest also joined the Eagles in the Premiership for the 1994–95 season after finishing second in Division One, while Middlesbrough could only manage ninth in Division One. Amazingly it was Crystal Palace's and Nottingham Forest's first season under the management of Alan Smith and Frank Clark respectively, while Bryan Robson left Manchester United to take charge of Middlesbrough when the 1993–94 season ended.

## ⚜ LIFE AFTER CLOUGHIE ⚜

After achieving promotion back to the Premiership at the first attempt, Nottingham Forest finished third in the Premiership table in 1994–95 to win a UEFA Cup slot, their first European campaign of the post-Heysel era. Frank Clarke's side was helped by the goalscoring exploits of their striker Stan Collymore, who netted 22 Premiership goals. However, Collymore left the City Ground at the end of the season and moved to Anfield for £8.5 million.

## ❧ O'LEARY SACKED ❧

When Leeds United met Cardiff City in the FA Cup third round in January 2002, the Yorkshire club sat at the top of the Premiership table. However, the Welsh club, placed mid-table in Division Two, caused a huge upset by beating Leeds United 2–1 at Ninian Park. Although Leeds finished fifth in the Premiership at the end of the season manager David O'Leary was sacked after four years in charge at Elland Road. Many people close to the club blamed O'Leary's book *Leeds United: On Trial* for the Irishman's departure, claiming that it destroyed morale in the dressing-room.

## ❧ NEW HOMES ❧

More than one-third of the Premiership clubs in 2007–08 played in stadiums less than a dozen years' old. This is the list:

| Stadium | Club | Opened |
| --- | --- | --- |
| Emirates | Arsenal | 2006 |
| Eastland (City of Manchester) | Manchester City | 2002 |
| JJB Stadium | Wigan Athletic | 1999 |
| Madejski Stadium | Reading | 1998 |
| Pride Park | Derby County | 1997 |
| Stadium of Light | Sunderland | 1997 |
| Reebok Stadium | Bolton Wanderers | 1997 |

## ❧ PAISLEY'S LAST BATTLE ❧

On 14 February 1996, the legendary Liverpool manager Bob Paisley died aged 77 after a four-year battle against cancer. Paisley won an astonishing 21 trophies between 1974 and 1983 and at the time of his death he was the most successful manager in English football. Sir Alex Ferguson has since taken over his mantle.

## ❧ GUNNERS GIVEN A LESSON IN STYLE ❧

On 25 February 2001, Manchester United annihilated their nearest challengers for the Premiership crown, Arsenal, 6–1 at Old Trafford.

## ❧ ROBBIE RICH ❧

On 1 November 1994, Liverpool handed Robbie Fowler, then aged 19, a contract that made him football's first teenage millionaire.

# ❧ 2007–08 BARCLAYS GOLDEN GLOVE AWARD ❧

This award was presented for the third successive season to Liverpool's Jose Reina, who kept 18 clean sheets in 38 Premiership games. David James – the all-time clean-sheet leader in Premier League history – came second with 17 clean sheets from 35 matches.

## ❧ SPURS HANDED RECORD FINE ❧

During the 1993–94 season, Tottenham Hotspur were the subject of a Football Association investigation that focused on financial irregularities that had occurred at the club during the 1980s when Irving Scholar had been the club's chairman. The club was found guilty and the FA handed out the heaviest financial penalty ever received by an English club, a fine of £600,000, deducted 12 Premiership points for the 1994–95 season and banned them from the 1994–95 FA Cup. Alan Sugar, the chairman of the club, appealed against the FA's ruling and succeeded in having it quashed – apart from the fine, which was increased to £1.5 million.

## ❧ QPR TOP DOGS IN THE CAPITAL ❧

Queen's Park Rangers, managed by former QPR and England captain Gerry Francis, ended the 1992–93 Premier League season in fifth place, highest of all the London clubs. Disappointingly for them, although fifth place was previously good enough for a UEFA Cup place, UEFA had not yet given back all of England's European competition places taken away following the 1985 Heysel disaster.

## ❧ RECORD-BUSTING RIO ❧

After losing their first Premiership campaign in four seasons in 2001–02, Manchester United broke the British record transfer fee in July 2002 by shelling out £29.1 million for Leeds United centre-half Rio Ferdinand. It made him the most expensive defender in the world, as well as Britain's most expensive player for the second time in two seasons.

## ❧ SPREADING THE SCORING ❧

Although 2000–01 Premier League champions Manchester United were also the league's top scorers with 79 goals, no United players were in the top five of the goalscoring charts at the season's end.

## ❧ OLD BOYS NETWORK ❧

The following table lists the 2007–08 Premier League clubs in order of seniority:

| Team | Founded | Age |
|---|---|---|
| Reading | 1871 | 136 |
| Aston Villa | 1874 | 133 |
| Bolton Wanderers | 1874 | 133 |
| Blackburn Rovers | 1875 | 132 |
| Birmingham City | 1875 | 132 |
| Middlesbrough | 1876 | 131 |
| Everton | 1878 | 129 |
| Manchester United | 1878 | 129 |
| Sunderland | 1879 | 128 |
| Fulham | 1879 | 128 |
| Manchester City | 1880 | 127 |
| Tottenham Hotspur | 1882 | 125 |
| Derby County | 1884 | 123 |
| Arsenal | 1886 | 121 |
| Liverpool | 1892 | 115 |
| Newcastle United | 1892 | 115 |
| West Ham United | 1895 | 112 |
| Portsmouth | 1898 | 109 |
| Chelsea | 1905 | 102 |
| Wigan Athletic | 1932 | 75 |

## ❧ FORZA ZOLA ❧

Chelsea's Gianfranco Zola was voted Player of the Year by both the Professional Footballers' Association and the Football Writers' Association in 1996–97, when he also helped the Blues to FA Cup success.

## ❧ SAINTLY BRILLIANCE ❧

In 1994–95 the unfancied Southampton surprised many football pundits by avoiding relegation to finish tenth in the Premier League, mostly thanks to the sheer brilliance of Matt Le Tissier. The Saints ended the campaign higher than more-fancied teams such as Chelsea (11th), Arsenal (12th) and Everton (15th). However, at the end of the season the Southampton manager Alan Ball packed his bags and took over at Manchester City, leaving long-serving coach Dave Merrington in charge at The Dell.

## ⚔ FINAL PREMIERSHIP TABLE 2002–2003 ⚔

| Pos | Team | P | W | D | L | F | A | Pts |
|-----|------|---|---|---|---|---|---|-----|
| 1. | Manchester United (C) | 38 | 25 | 8 | 5 | 74 | 34 | 83 |
| 2. | Arsenal | 38 | 23 | 9 | 6 | 85 | 42 | 78 |
| 3. | Newcastle United | 38 | 21 | 6 | 11 | 63 | 48 | 69 |
| 4. | Chelsea | 38 | 19 | 10 | 9 | 68 | 38 | 67 |
| 5. | Liverpool | 38 | 18 | 10 | 10 | 61 | 41 | 64 |
| 6. | Blackburn Rovers | 38 | 16 | 12 | 10 | 52 | 43 | 60 |
| 7. | Everton | 38 | 17 | 8 | 13 | 48 | 49 | 59 |
| 8. | Southampton | 38 | 13 | 13 | 12 | 43 | 46 | 52 |
| 9. | Manchester City | 38 | 15 | 6 | 17 | 47 | 54 | 51 |
| 10. | Tottenham | 38 | 14 | 8 | 16 | 51 | 62 | 50 |
| 11. | Middlesbrough | 38 | 13 | 10 | 15 | 48 | 44 | 49 |
| 12. | Charlton Athletic | 38 | 14 | 7 | 17 | 45 | 56 | 49 |
| 13. | Birmingham City | 38 | 13 | 9 | 16 | 41 | 49 | 48 |
| 14. | Fulham | 38 | 13 | 9 | 16 | 41 | 50 | 48 |
| 15. | Leeds United | 38 | 14 | 5 | 19 | 58 | 57 | 47 |
| 16. | Aston Villa | 38 | 12 | 9 | 17 | 42 | 47 | 45 |
| 17. | Bolton Wanderers | 38 | 10 | 14 | 14 | 41 | 51 | 44 |
| 18. | West Ham United (R) | 38 | 10 | 12 | 16 | 42 | 59 | 42 |
| 19. | West Bromwich Albion (R) | 38 | 6 | 8 | 24 | 29 | 65 | 26 |
| 20. | Sunderland (R) | 38 | 4 | 7 | 27 | 21 | 65 | 19 |

## ⚔ THAT'S ENTERTAINMENT ⚔

A highlight of the 2007–08 season was an exhilarating encounter at Fratton Park in which Portsmouth beat Reading 7–4, with Benjani Mwaruwari scoring a hat-trick for Portsmouth. Although the 11-goal aggregate was a Premiership record for a single match, the total could have been higher still. During the game Marcus Hahnemann, Reading's American goalkeeper, saved a point-blank shot from Glen Johnson; David James in the Pompey goal saved a penalty from Nicky Shorey; and a goal was disallowed for offside. Benjani only played because Kanu was injured.

## ⚔ RACE TO STAY UP ⚔

Bolton Wanderers, Manchester City and Queen's Park Rangers were relegated from the Premier League in 1995–96. City needed to beat Liverpool in their final game, but somehow the wrong message went out to the players, who appeared to be playing for a draw late in the match, thinking a single point would be good enough for survival.

## ❧ JEEPERS KEEPERS ❧

On 14 October 2006, Chelsea goalkeepers Petr Cech and Carlo Cudicini both sustained head injuries during their match against Reading. Cech underwent surgery for a depressed skull fracture, while the more fortunate Cudicini was treated and released from hospital the same evening.

## ❧ UNITED KEANE TO BREAK THE BANK ❧

Before the start of the 1993–94 season, Roy Keane became the most expensive player in British football history. The Nottingham Forest and Republic of Ireland hard man left relegated Nottingham Forest and joined the reigning Premier League champions, Manchester United, for a fee of £3.75 million. The 22-year-old had turned down offers from Arsenal and Blackburn Rovers to join Alex Ferguson's exciting side.

## ❧ INTERNATIONAL EAGLES ❧

In season 1997–98 Crystal Palace added internationals Michele Padovano (Italy) and Tomas Brolin (Sweden) to their team, which already had the Italian Attilio Lombardo in the heart of their midfield. However, the international trio could not save Palace from a quick return to Division One. Lombardo had enjoyed considerable success in Italian football, winning the the European Cup Winners' Cup (1990), Coppa Italia (1991 and 1994), Serie A (1991) and the Supercoppa Italia (1991) during his time with Sampdoria (1989–95). With Juventus (1995–97) he won the UEFA Champions League (1996), the World Club Championship (1996) and the European Super Cup (1996).

## ❧ OLD BOYS REUNION ❧

In December 1998, Brian Kidd left his assistant manager's job under Alex Ferguson at Manchester United and took charge of Blackburn Rovers, who had sacked manager Roy Hodgson in November. Kidd brought former Manchester United hero Brian McClair to Ewood Park from Motherwell as his assistant. In his first month at Blackburn, Kidd won the Premier League Manager of the Month Award, but Rovers were relegated to Division One after drawing 0–0 with Manchester United at Ewood Park in their penultimate game of the season.

## ❧ PREMIERSHIP TALK (16) ❧

"My best moment? I have a lot of good moments, but the one I prefer is when I kicked the hooligan."
*Eric Cantona (Manchester United)*

## ❧ GIGGSY HITS CENTURY ❧

When Ryan Giggs scored Manchester United's opening goal in their 4–1 win over Derby County in the Premier League at Old Trafford on 8 December 2007, it was his 100th league goal for the Red Devils. Derby's goal was their first in nine Premiership away games, in which they had conceded 24 goals.

## ❧ "JUDAS" SIGNS FOR THE REDS ❧

Prior to the start of the 2000–01 season, Nick Barmby became the first Everton player in more than 40 years to move across Stanley Park, when he joined the Reds in a £6m transfer deal. At the time Barmby claimed he loved Liverpool more than Everton, which angered Blues fans. In the Merseyside derby on 29 October 2000 Barmby ran out at Anfield to cries of "Judas!" from the Everton fans. Barmby silenced the Blues by scoring in a 3–1 win for Liverpool. In August 2002, Barmby was sold for £2.75 million to Leeds United.

## ❧ WISE MOVE ❧

David May left Blackburn Rovers prior to the start of the 1994–95 season and joined Manchester United. His move may not have looked like a good decision at the end of the season when Rovers pipped United to the Premiership title, but May went on to have a successful career with United, one that saw him win many trophies including the famous Treble in 1999.

## ❧ HOULLIER WALKS ALONE ❧

Liverpool brought in the former French national coach Gerard Houllier at the start of the 1998–99 season to act as joint manager of the club alongside Roy Evans. However, Evans was unhappy with the arrangement and quit in November 1998. The Anfield club could only manage seventh place in the Premiership in 1998–99, which was the club's worst league finish in five years and not good enough to secure European football.

## ❦ ANCIENT MONUMENTS ❦

Eleven Premiership clubs in 2007–08 had played at the same home ground for more than 100 years: They were:

| Club | Stadium | Year Built |
|------|---------|------------|
| Blackburn Rovers | Ewood Park | 1882 |
| Liverpool | Anfield | 1884 |
| Everton | Goodison Park | 1892 |
| Newcastle United | St James' Park | 1892 |
| Fulham | Craven Cottage | 1896 |
| Aston Villa | Villa Park | 1897 |
| Portsmouth | Fratton Park | 1898 |
| Tottenham Hotspur | White Hart Lane | 1899 |
| West Ham United | Upton Park | 1904 |
| Birmingham City | St Andrews | 1905 |
| Chelsea | Stamford Bridge | 1905 |

## ❦ POMPEY'S GREAT ESCAPE ❦

With ten games remaining in the 2005–06 Premiership season, it seemed certain that Portsmouth would be relegated. They were eight points from safety, but following the return of manager Harry Redknapp they strung together a series of good results to steer them to safety at the expense of West Bromwich Albion and Birmingham City with a game to go (Sunderland's fate was already sealed).

## ❦ SPEAKING OUT ❦

In August 2006, Leeds United chairman Ken Bates, formerly the chairman of Chelsea, reported the London club to the Football Association, the FA Premier League and FIFA over the alleged tapping-up of three Leeds youth-team players.

## ❦ CHELSEA'S TREBLE ❦

In 1995–96 Chelsea finished 11th for the third time in four seasons.

## ❦ PREMIERSHIP TALK (17) ❦

"We have top players and, sorry if I'm arrogant, we have a top manager."
*Former Chelsea manager **Jose Mourinho***

## ❧ WALK-OUT FOR THE SPECIAL ONE ❧

At half-time during Chelsea's 0–0 draw with Fulham in the Premiership on 29 September 2007, a number of Chelsea fans walked out of Stamford Bridge in protest over Jose Mourinho's departure from the club.

## ❧ THE LITTLE FELLA ❧

In October 1995, Bryan Robson paid Sao Paulo £4.75 million for the services of their diminutive 22-year-old Brazilian striker Juninho Paulista. Juninho was an instant success at the Riverside Stadium and went on to inscribe his name in the club's history books as one of their greatest-ever players. Juninho stood just 1.67 metres tall and during his time on Teeside became known to Boro fans as "TLF (The Little Fella)".

## ❧ BACK IN WORK ❧

In September 1996, Howard Wilkinson was sacked as the manager of Leeds United after suffering a 4–0 home defeat at the hands of Manchester United. George Graham, himself sacked as the manager of Arsenal on 21 February 1995, took over the reins at Elland Road. Graham had been banned by the FA for a year after he admitted having accepted a "bung" from the Norwegian football agent Rune Hauge.

## ❧ WENGER MISCALCULATES SHIFT IN POWER ❧

When Arsenal, the defending Premiership champions, enjoyed a good start to the 2002–03 Premier League season, their manager Arsene Wenger talked about a shift in power from Manchester to North London. However, Sir Alex Ferguson's side made the Frenchman rue his words by reclaiming the Premiership crown at the end of the season with Arsenal finishing runners-up to United for the fourth time in five seasons.

## ❧ GOD ARRIVES AT ANFIELD ❧

Robbie Fowler, aged 18, scored in his first-team debut for Liverpool, a 3–1 League Cup first-round, first-leg win over Fulham at Craven Cottage on 22 September 1993. He went on to score 12 Premiership goals in 28 games that season. Reds fans later nicknamed him "God".

# ⚘ AFRICAN PREMIER LEAGUE FANTASY XI ⚘

**1**
Bruce
*GROBBELAAR*
*(ZIMBABWE)*

**2**
Emmanuel
*EBOUE*
*(IVORY COAST)*

**6**
Lucas
*RADEBE*
*(SOUTH AFRICA, capt.)*

**5**
Christopher
*SAMBA*
*(REP. OF CONGO)*

**3**
Kolo
*TOURE*
*(IVORY COAST)*

**7**
El Hadji-
*DIOUF*
*(SENEGAL)*

**4**
Michael
*ESSIEN*
*(GHANA)*

**8**
Mohammed
*SISSOKO*
*(MALI)*

**9**
George
*WEAH*
*(LIBERIA)*

**10**
Didier
*DROGBA*
*(IVORY COAST)*

**11**
JJ
*OKOCHA*
*(NIGERIA)*

*Substitutes*
Radhi *JAIDE (Tunisia)* • Freddie *KANOUTE (Mali)* • Benni *McCARTHY (S. Africa)*
*YAKUBU* Aiyebbeni *(Nigeria)* • Quinton *FORTUNE (S. Africa)*

*Manager*
John *FASHANU*
*(English but of Yoruba Nigerian descent on his father's side)*

### *Did You Know That?*
In November 1994 John Fashanu and Bruce Grobbelaar were accused of match fixing along with Hans Segers and a Malaysian businessman named Heng Suan Lim.

## ⚘ PREMIER MEDAL COLLECTOR ⚘

Manchester United's Ryan Giggs has won more Premier League winners' medals, ten, than any other player (1993, 1994, 1996, 1997, 1999, 2000, 2001, 2003, 2007 & 2008). United's ninth Premiership crown in 2006–07 also placed Giggs as the all-time leading medal winner in English top flight, passing the eight First Division winners' medals collected by Alan Hansen with Liverpool.

## ⚘ LITTLE BIG MAN ⚘

In 1995–96 Brian Little guided Aston Villa to League Cup glory and fourth place in the Premiership.

## ❧ THEIR BEST FINISHES ❧

The following table lists each 2007–08 Premier League club's best-ever finish in English football's top flight:

| Pos | Team | Highest Placing | Champions |
|---|---|---|---|
| 1. | Liverpool | Champions | 18 times |
| 2. | Manchester United* | Champions | 17 times |
| 3. | Arsenal* | Champions | 13 times |
| 4. | Everton | Champions | 9 times |
| 5. | Aston Villa | Champions | 7 times |
| 6. | Sunderland | Champions | 6 times |
| 7. | Newcastle United | Champions | 4 times |
| =8. | Blackburn Rovers* | Champions | 3 times |
| =8. | Chelsea* | Champions | 3 times |
| =10. | Derby County | Champions | 2 times |
| =10. | Manchester City | Champions | 2 times |
| =10. | Portsmouth | Champions | 2 times |
| =10. | Tottenham Hotspur | Champions | 2 times |
| 14. | Bolton Wanderers | Third (3 times) | |
| =15. | Middlesbrough | Third (1913–14) | |
| =15. | West Ham United | Third (1985–86) | |
| 17. | Birmingham City | Sixth (1955–56) | |
| 18. | Reading | Eighth (2006–07) | |
| 19. | Fulham | Ninth (2003–04) | |
| 20. | Wigan Athletic | Tenth (2005–06) | |

*\* First Division & Premier League champions*

## ❧ A RUUD DEPARTURE ❧

On 12 February 1998, Chelsea sacked their manager Ruud Gullit following a bust-up between the Dutch superstar and the club's chairman Ken Bates. Gianluca Vialli, their 33-year-old Italian striker, took charge of first-team affairs as player-manager. Over the next three months Vialli guided the Blues to victory in both the Coca-Cola Cup and the European Cup Winners' Cup. The Italian theme continued in the Premiership during the 1997–98 season: when Steve Coppell vacated his position as manager of Crystal Palace, moving upstairs to be director of football at Selhurst Park, he was replaced by the Eagles' 31-year-old midfielder Attilio Lombardo as player-manager (along with Tomas Brolin). However, the Brolin/Lombardo tenure only lasted until the end of the season, when Terry Venables took charge.

## ❧ A NEW SHERIFF AT THE BRIDGE ❧

On 13 December 2007, Avram Grant, aged 52, signed a four-year contract with Chelsea. The Israeli had taken charge at Stamford Bridge in September 2007 after Jose Mourinho's departure. Following his first game in charge of the Blues, a 2–0 Premiership defeat away to Manchester United, Chelsea went on a 16-game unbeaten run.

## ❧ THE TINKERMAN IS TINKERED WITH ❧

After guiding Chelsea to the semi-finals of the UEFA Champions League and runners-up position in the Premier League in season 2003–04, the Blues' highest league finish since their 1955 title, Claudio Ranieri was rewarded with the sack. The man nicknamed the "Tinkerman" by the English media was replaced by Jose Mourinho.

## ❧ NO WAY TO TREAT A KNIGHT ❧

At the end of August 2004, just four games into the season, Newcastle United sacked manager Sir Bobby Robson and replaced him with the Blackburn Rovers manager Graeme Souness.

## ❧ HELICOPTER CRASH ❧

On 22 October 1996, Chelsea director Matthew Harding, aged 42, died along with four other people when their helicopter crashed on their way home from a Premiership game that the Blues lost 2–1 at Bolton.

## ❧ QUEEN'S APPOINTMENT ❧

On 24 November 1993, the Queens Park Rangers manager, Gerry Francis, was tipped to take over from Graham Taylor as England manager after Taylor quit his post as the national team boss following England's failure to qualify for the 1994 World Cup finals. However, Francis was overlooked in favour of a former QPR manager, Terry Venables.

## ❧ SIR ALEX THE GREAT ❧

In the 2002–03 season Sir Alex Ferguson won the Barclaycard Manager of the Year Award after guiding Manchester United to their eighth Premiership title.

## ♔ PREMIERSHIP TALK (18) ♕

"Sometimes in football you have to score goals."
*Thierry Henry (Arsenal)*

## ♔ HAPPY 125TH BIRTHDAY ♕

Prior to their home game against Aston Villa at White Hart Lane on 1 October 2007, Tottenham Hotspur celebrated their 125th anniversary with a parade of legends before kick-off. However, the Villains looked set to burst Spurs' party bubble when they took a 4–1 lead after going a goal down. But Spurs fought back and scored three more goals to earn a point from the 4–4 thriller leaving them two places off the foot of the Premiership table after eight games of the season had been played.

## ♔ NEW BHOY IN TOWN ♕

Martin O'Neill resigned as manager of Leicester City after guiding them to eighth in the Premiership (their best finish since the league was formed) and League Cup glory at Wembley (for the second time during his reign) at the end of the 1999–2000 season. He moved north of the border to take charge at Glasgow Celtic. The Bhoys achieved much success under O'Neill's astute leadership. Peter Taylor left Gillingham to succeed O'Neill at Leicester.

## ♔ TRUE CONFESSIONS ♕

In November 1994, Paul Merson, the Arsenal and England midfielder, broke down before the television cameras and admitted that he was an alcoholic as well as being hooked on cocaine and gambling. Merson took a three-month sabbatical from the game and underwent a drug rehabilitation programme.

## ♔ THE SPECIAL ONE LIVES UP TO HIS NAME ♕

Jose Mourinho, nicknamed the "Special One", lived up to the tag in his first season in charge of Chelsea, guiding the Blues to the Premier League title. It was Chelsea's first Championship success since they won the First Division in 1955. Chelsea were in superb form all season, and hardly any team could live with them as they racked up a Premiership record of 95 points (29 wins, 8 draws and 1 defeat) and a unique defensive record of only 15 league goals conceded.

# � AUSTRALIA PREMIER LEAGUE FANTASY XI ✥

**1**
Mark
*SCHWARZER*
*(MIDDLESBROUGH)*

**2**
Brett
*EMERTON*
*(BLACKBURN)*

**6**
Hayden
*FOXE*
*(WEST HAM)*

**5**
Craig
*MOORE*
*(NEWCASTLE UTD)*

**3**
Lucas
*NEILL*
*(WEST HAM) (capt)*

**7**
Luke
*WILKSHIRE*
*(MIDDLESBROUGH)*

**4**
Danny
*TIATTO*
*(MAN CITY)*

**8**
Stan
*LAZARIDIS*
*(BIRMINGHAM)*

**9**
Tim
*CAHILL*
*(EVERTON)*

**10**
Mark
*VIDUKA*
*(NEWCASTLE UTD)*

**11**
Harry
*KEWELL*
*(LIVERPOOL)*

### Substitutes
Mark *BOSNICH* *(ASTON VILLA)* • Robbie *SLATER* *(SOUTHAMPTON)* •
Josip *SKOKO* *(WIGAN)* • Tony *VIDMAR* *(MIDDLESBROUGH)* • Paul *OKON* *(MIDDLESBROUGH)*

### Manager
Terry *VENABLES*

### *Did You Know That?*
Terry Venables became manager of Australia in November 1996, and almost took the side to the 1998 World Cup finals – Australia lost their final play-off match against Iran on away goals.

## � GUNNERS ON THE MOVE ✥

At the end of Arsenal's 2001–02 Double-winning season their chairman Peter Hill-Wood announced that the club would move into its new 60,000-capacity, all-seater stadium at the start of the 2004–05 season.

## ✥ BACK IN THE FIZZ ✥

At the end of the 2006–07 Premier League season, two of the three promoted clubs, Sheffield United and Watford, dropped back into the Coca-Cola Championship along with Charlton Athletic, whose eight-year Premiership tenure came to an end.

## ❦ FINAL PREMIERSHIP TABLE 2003–2004 ❦

| Pos Team | P | W | D | L | F | A | Pts |
|---|---|---|---|---|---|---|---|
| 1. Arsenal (C) | 38 | 26 | 12 | 0 | 73 | 26 | 90 |
| 2. Chelsea | 38 | 24 | 7 | 7 | 67 | 30 | 79 |
| 3. Manchester United | 38 | 23 | 6 | 9 | 64 | 35 | 75 |
| 4. Liverpool | 38 | 16 | 12 | 10 | 55 | 37 | 60 |
| 5. Newcastle United | 38 | 13 | 17 | 8 | 52 | 40 | 56 |
| 6. Aston Villa | 38 | 15 | 11 | 12 | 48 | 44 | 56 |
| 7. Charlton Athletic | 38 | 14 | 11 | 13 | 51 | 51 | 53 |
| 8. Bolton Wanderers | 38 | 14 | 11 | 13 | 48 | 56 | 53 |
| 9. Fulham | 38 | 14 | 10 | 14 | 52 | 46 | 52 |
| 10. Birmingham City | 38 | 12 | 14 | 12 | 43 | 48 | 50 |
| 11. Middlesbrough | 38 | 13 | 9 | 16 | 44 | 52 | 48 |
| 12. Southampton | 38 | 12 | 11 | 15 | 44 | 45 | 47 |
| 13. Portsmouth | 38 | 12 | 9 | 17 | 47 | 54 | 45 |
| 14. Tottenham Hotspur | 38 | 13 | 6 | 19 | 47 | 57 | 45 |
| 15. Blackburn Rovers | 38 | 12 | 8 | 18 | 51 | 59 | 44 |
| 16. Manchester City | 38 | 9 | 14 | 15 | 55 | 54 | 41 |
| 17. Everton | 38 | 9 | 12 | 17 | 45 | 57 | 39 |
| 18. Leicester City (R) | 38 | 6 | 15 | 17 | 48 | 65 | 33 |
| 19. Leeds United (R) | 38 | 8 | 9 | 21 | 40 | 79 | 33 |
| 20. Wolverhampton Wanderers (R) | 38 | 7 | 12 | 19 | 38 | 77 | 33 |

## ❦ NO CHRISTMAS CHEER FOR LAWRIE ❦

On 21 December 2007, Fulham sacked their manager, Lawrie Sanchez, who had only taken over the club from Chris Coleman in April 2007 (originally on a caretaker basis). He became the seventh Premier League manager to leave or be removed from his post in the 2007–08 season. The club were struggling in 18th place in the Premiership, having won just two games all season.

## ❦ CRAZY GANGS HIT LOW ❦

Wimbledon finished 14th in the Premiership in 1995–96, their lowest placing since joining the big guns a decade earlier.

## ❦ LAST GOAL STANDING ❦

Julian Dicks was the last Liverpool player to score in front of the standing Kop. On 9 April 1994 Dicks converted a penalty in Liverpool's 1–0 Premiership win over Ipswich Town. (117)

## ❧ SOLE CASUALTY ❧

Bolton Wanderers' Roy McFarland was the only Premiership manager to lose his job during the 1995–96 season, although Southampton's Dave Merrington, who had helped the Saints avoid the drop, was also relieved of his duties in June 1996.

## ❧ WOEFUL CITY ❧

Of the clubs newly promoted to the Premiership at the start of the 2000–01 season Manchester City was the only one to suffer relegation back to Division One at the end of it. It was the Blues' fourth relegation in a seven-year period that had also seen them fall into Division Two for a season. Shortly afterwards, they sacked their manager Joe Royle.

## ❧ EVERY GAME PLAYED AWAY ❧

During the 2002–03 season Fulham played their home games at Queen's Park Rangers' Loftus Road ground as Craven Cottage was being upgraded. Loftus Road witnessed the lowest Premier League attendance of the season when a crowd of 14,017 paid to see Fulham play Blackburn Rovers.

## ❧ SKY BLUES HIT ORBIT ❧

Going into the 1994–95 season Coventry City made Manchester United's Dion Dublin their record transfer purchase at £2 million to take him from Old Trafford to Highfield Road.

## ❧ QUICK OFF THE MARK ❧

Robbie Fowler scored the fastest ever Premier League hat-trick when he bagged three against Arsenal at Anfield on 28 August 1994 in only four minutes and 33 seconds, just before the half-hour mark. Liverpool won the game 3–0.

## ❧ SEVENTH HEAVEN FOR BLACK CATS ❧

Sunderland finished seventh in the Premiership table in the 2000–01 season for the second year in a row. The Black Cats looked on course for at least a UEFA Cup place when they were lying second behind Manchester United in early February, but they fell away at the end.

# ⚜ MICHAEL OWEN ⚜

Michael James Owen was born on 14 December 1979 in Hawarden, Cheshire. His father Terry played for Everton, so it was no surprise that Michael grew up supporting Everton, nor that his boyhood hero was Everton and England striker Gary Lineker. When he was seven years old, his dad persuaded the manager of Mold Alexandra to allow Michael to play for their team, an Under-11 side. Michael signed schoolboy forms with Liverpool aged 13 and attended Lilleshall's School of Excellence. As a 16-year-old he was in Liverpool's FA Youth Cup-winning team and, just after his 17th birthday, Michael signed professional terms with the Reds.

In May 1997, Michael made his Liverpool debut against Wimbledon, scoring in a 2–1 defeat. He was a regular starter in 1997–98 following an injury to Robbie Fowler and ended his first Premiership season as the club's joint top scorer with 18 goals. Not surprisingly, Michael was voted the 1997–98 PFA Young Player of the Year, to say nothing of a sensational arrival on the international scene at the 1998 World Cup finals. After 23 goals in 40 games for Liverpool in 1998–99, a niggling hamstring injury made the following season one to forget. But, in 2000–01, he helped Liverpool to League Cup, UEFA Cup and FA Cup success, scoring both of Liverpool's goals in their 2–1 FA Cup win over Arsenal.

Michael won FA Charity Shield and European Super Cup winners' medals in 2001–02 while, on a personal note, he became the first English player since Kevin Keegan to win the coveted Ballon d'Or, the European Footballer of the Year Award. On 21 December 2001, he scored his 100th goal for Liverpool, before going on to bag his 100th Premier League goal for Liverpool the following season.

On 13 August 2004, Michael joined Real Madrid for £8 million, but the move was not a huge success, though he scored 16 times in 41 outings, many as a substitute. He returned to England a year later, becoming Newcastle United's record signing, the club paying £16 million for him. He scored his first goal for the Magpies in his second game for the club, but a series of injuries limited his appearances, including the cruciate knee-ligament injury he suffered on England duty at the 2006 World Cup finals. On the international front Michael has scored 40 goals in 88 games for England (up to the end of 2007–08).

### *Did You Know That?*
One week after scoring for Liverpool against Oliver Kahn of Bayern Munich in the 2001 European Super Cup, Michael bagged a hat-trick against him in England's 5–1 win over Germany in Munich.

## ❧ JAMES BOND ROLE AT NEWCASTLE ❧

On 1 October 2007, Newcastle United strenuously denied claims made in a Sunday national tabloid newspaper of a bugging scandal within the club. The newspaper published claims by Brian Tough, a former security consultant for the club who was initially hired as a bodyguard for Douglas Hall, the son of the Magpies' one-time owner Sir John Hall. Tough claimed that he was paid £40,000 a year to bug the phones of former manager Kevin Keegan, former Sunderland chairman Bob Murray and others. Freddy Shepherd, who was chairman at St James' Park at the time when the bugging was alleged to have taken place, denied any involvement in the allegations, saying: "This is James Bond stuff. I certainly didn't employ anyone in 007 activities at St James' Park. Mr Tough was never employed by me or the club." A club spokesman added: "If the club has been the victim of any criminal activity, the club will take appropriate action."

## ❧ GROUND SHARE OPPOSTION ❧

During the 2001–02 season, Everton announced plans to move away from their Goodison Park home and relocate to a brand new all-seater stadium with a 55,000 capacity on the banks of the River Mersey. There was talk of a ground share with Liverpool, leading to fans of both clubs jamming radio phone-ins with their vociferous objections to any such partnership. One Everton fan went on the air and said he wouldn't share a Twix with a Liverpool fan, never mind a football stadium.

## ❧ LAST-GASP SIGNING ❧

On 31 August 2002, the date of the transfer deadline, Robbie Keane left Leeds United and joined Tottenham Hotspur.

## ❧ ARCH RIVAL TAKES CHARGE AT THE LANE ❧

In September 1998 Tottenham Hotspur sacked manager Christian Gross, who had been in charge at White Hart Lane for less than a year. A month later Spurs appointed the former Arsenal and Leeds manager George Graham as his replacement. The golden touch that Graham enjoyed at Arsenal as manager returned in his first season in charge of Spurs as he guided the team to League Cup success and only their second European campaign since 1985.

# ❦ THE FOREIGN INVASION ❦

At the start of the 2007–08 Premier League season a total of 330 foreign players were registered as first-team players with the 20 Premiership clubs. This equates to 16.5 foreign players per Premiership team and, as the table below shows, only three teams still had more English players than foreign ones.

| Team | No. of English players | No. of foreign players |
| --- | --- | --- |
| Arsenal | 2 | 23 |
| Liverpool | 4 | 20 |
| Blackburn Rovers | 5 | 20 |
| Manchester City | 5 | 16 |
| Birmingham City | 6 | 17 |
| Bolton Wanderers | 7 | 18 |
| Chelsea | 7 | 17 |
| Fulham | 7 | 21 |
| Reading | 8 | 15 |
| Sunderland | 8 | 18 |
| Everton | 9 | 18 |
| Middlesbrough | 9 | 12 |
| Portsmouth | 9 | 15 |
| Newcastle United | 10 | 18 |
| Wigan Athletic | 10 | 14 |
| Manchester United | 11 | 17 |
| Tottenham Hotspur | 11 | 17 |
| Aston Villa | 12 | 10 |
| Derby County | 16 | 13 |
| West Ham United | 16 | 13 |

## Did You Know That?

In November 2007, UEFA president Michel Platini attacked the Premier League's foreign scouting policy: "I am against this philosophy. We need to take care of the identity of the club. I don't like the system that scours other countries for the best young talent to bring back to their team."

# ❦ ASHES FEVER ❦

A number of clubs reported drops in attendance during the 2005–06 season and cited cricket fever following England's Ashes victory over Australia as the main reason for the slump.

## CITY FEELING THE BLUES

At the end of the 1997–98 season, Manchester City (who had been in the Premier League between 1992 and 1997) were relegated for the second time in successive seasons, dropping from Premiership football to Division Two. City went into their final game of the season, against Stoke City at Stoke's new Britannia Stadium, knowing that a win for either team might see them avoid relegation. In fact Man City beat Stoke City 5–2, but both clubs were relegated (along with bottom-placed Reading) because the three teams above the drop zone all won their games. It was the first time in the club's history that the Citizens suffered relegation to the third tier of the English Football League, and their fans, together with the Stoke City fans, marked their last day in Division One with disgraceful violence after the game.

## A NEW HOME

Middlesbrough, First Division champions in 1994–95, went into the 1995–96 season with a new home. The club left Ayresome Park and moved to the purpose-built Riverside Stadium, the first new stadium in English football's top flight in 72 years.

## LEEDS SMASH CLUB'S PIGGY BANK

In November 2000, Leeds United broke the English transfer record when they handed over £18 million to West Ham United for their 22-year-old centre-half Rio Ferdinand. The previous record was set by Newcastle United in January 1995 when they forked out £15 million to Blackburn Rovers for Alan Shearer, and the Geordies' spending was equalled by Chelsea in May 2000 when they brought Jimmy Floyd Hasselbaink to Stamford Bridge from Atletico Madrid.

## UNLUCKY TOFFEES

On the final day of the 2001–02 season, David Moyes' first full season in charge at Goodison Park, Everton were in contention for a top-six finish and with it a UEFA Cup place in season 2003–04. However, they lost their last game of the season to the champions, Manchester United, 2–1 at Goodison Park. The defeat saw Everton finish seventh in the table, and European qualification went to Blackburn Rovers, who finished one point above them.

# ❦ NORDIC PREMIER LEAGUE FANTASY XI ❦

**1**
Peter
*SCHMEICHEL*
*(DENMARK)*

**2**
Daniel
*AGGER*
*(DENMARK)*

**6**
Olof
*MELBERG*
*(SWEDEN, capt.)*

**5**
Ronny
*JOHNSEN*
*(NORWAY)*

**3**
John Arne
*RIISE*
*(NORWAY)*

**7**
Jari
*LITMANEN*
*(FINLAND)*

**4**
Jan
*MOLBY*
*(DENMARK)*

**8**
Eidur
*GUDJOHNSEN*
*(ICELAND)*

**10**
Ole Gunnar
*SOLSKJAER*
*(NORWAY)*

**9**
Tore Andre
*FLO*
*(NORWAY)*

**11**
Jesper
*BLOMQVIST*
*(SWEDEN)*

*Substitutes*
Thomas *SORENSEN (Denmark)* • Stig Inge *BJØRNEBYE (Norway)*
Sami *HYPPIA (Finland)* • Mikael *FORRSSEL (Finland)*
Henrik *LARSSON (Sweden)*
*Manager*
Egil *OLSEN (Norway)*

***Did You Know That?***
Egil Olsen took Norway to the FIFA World Cup finals in 1994
and 1998.

## ❦ BLUES' EUROPEAN HAT-TRICK ❦

Chelsea's player-manager Gianluca Vialli guided the Blues to third
place in the Premiership and European Super Cup glory in. At
the end of the season the 35-year-old Italian hung up his boots to
concentrate on coaching. Third-place (and a place in the Champions
League play-offs) secured a third-consecutive season of European
football for the Stamford Bridge outfit.

## ❦ OSSIE GETS THE BOOT ❦

Tottenham Hotspur sacked Ossie Ardiles as manager in November
1995 after they lost 3–0 to Notts County in the League Cup. Spurs
appointed QPR's former manager Gerry Francis as their new boss.

## ❦ PREMIERSHIP TALK (19) ❧

"Football must be your priority. You don't need to live in London or Manchester to be happy; you don't need to be surrounded by expensive shops or fancy cafes. What's your priority – your wife and her shopping or your football? Or money? If a player doesn't want to come to Sunderland because his wife wants to go shopping in London, it's a sad state of affairs."
*Roy Keane, Sunderland manager, August 2007*

## ❦ ALMOST A RUUD SIGNING ❧

In the summer of 2000 Manchester United, the reigning champions, announced that the coveted PSV Eindhoven and Dutch international striker Ruud van Nistelrooy was set to join the Old Trafford side. However, van Nistelrooy subsequently failed a medical as a result of a knee injury and his move was put on hold for a year. Meanwhile Sir Alex Ferguson did get the United chequebook out and paid AS Monaco £7.8 million, a club record transfer fee for a goalkeeper, for the French 1998 World Cup winner Fabian Barthez.

## ❦ LIVERPOOL SLUMP ❧

Entering 2003 Liverpool lay sixth in the Premiership table, streets behind the eventual champions Manchester United, while their manager Gerard Houllier was suffering the worst run a Liverpool manager had had for almost half a century. In the end the Anfield side finished fifth in the table and outside the UEFA Champions League places.

## ❦ FIVE TROPHIES NOT GOOD ENOUGH ❧

At the start of the 2000–01 season Chelsea sacked manager Gianluca Vialli, despite the fact that the former Italian international striker had won five trophies since his appointment as player-manager in February 1998. Indeed, the fifth trophy was the 2001 FA Charity Shield victory over Manchester United in the last ever club game at Wembley Stadium before it was torn down and rebuilt.

## ❦ FOUR FROM FIVE FOR FERGIE ❧

In 1996–97 Alex Ferguson guided Manchester United to their fourth Premiership title in five seasons.

## ❧ THE VERY BIG BOYS ❧

The tallest players in the Premier League during the 2007–08 season were:

| | | | |
|---|---|---|---|
| 1. | Peter Crouch | Liverpool | 200cm (6ft 7ins) |
| =2. | Asmir Begovic | Portsmouth | 199cm (6ft 6ins) |
| =2. | Andreas Isaksson | Manchester City | 199cm (6ft 6ins) |
| =2. | Zat Knight | Aston Villa | 199cm (6ft 6ins) |

## ❧ EUELL DO NICELY ❧

Charlton Athletic broke the club's record transfer fee at the end of the 2000–01 season when they paid First Division Wimbledon £4.75 million for their highly prized striker Jason Euell. Throughout his career Euell, who is deaf in his left ear, has been a role model for many children who share his problem. Indeed, he has been an ambassador for the National Deaf Awareness in Sport Alliance since 2000 and is very active for the charity, taking part in various fundraising events.

## ❧ BANTAMS PUNCH ABOVE THEIR WEIGHT ❧

On the final day of the 1999–2000 Premiership season Bradford City played Liverpool at Valley Parade. Liverpool needed a victory to secure UEFA Champions League football, while the Bantams needed to win to retain their Premiership status. Bradford City, playing in English football's top flight for the first time since 1922, beat Liverpool 1–0 thanks to a goal from their defender David Weatherall. In the end Bradford beat the drop by three points, while Liverpool lost the third UEFA Champions League slot to Leeds United by two points.

## ❧ SIR BOBBY'S TOON ❧

In the 2001–02 season, Sir Bobby Robson guided Newcastle United to fourth in the Premiership table, their highest placing since 1997, and secured UEFA Champions League football for only the second time in the club's history.

## ❧ PIPPED AT THE POST ❧

Arsenal claimed the last UEFA Cup slot on the final day of the 1995–96 season by two points from Everton.

## ❧ WALTER'S REIGN ❧

In his first season in charge of Everton, Walter Smith guided the Merseyside club to 14th in the Premiership table. Prior to Smith's arrival at Goodison Park, he guided Glasgow Rangers to seven Scottish championships, three Scottish FA Cups and four Scottish League Cups.

## ❧ FROM SINNERS TO SAINTS ❧

Arsene Wenger's Arsenal sides have often been heavily criticized for their indiscipline, receiving 52 red cards from season 1996–97 to 2002–03. However, the sinners became saints in seasons 2003–04 and 2004–05, winning the Premier League's Fair Play League tables for sporting behaviour.

## ❧ PREMIERSHIP TALK (20) ❧

"Buying players for Chelsea is the hardest job in the Premier League."
*Former Chelsea manager* **Jose Mourinho**

## ❧ BLUES AND REDS CLEAN UP ❧

With Manchester United and Chelsea making a clean sweep of the 2006–07 season's domestic silverware (United won the Premier League title, while Chelsea won the League Cup and the FA Cup) it meant that Spurs (fifth), Everton (sixth) and Bolton Wanderers (seventh) all claimed UEFA Cup places for the 2007–08 season. Blackburn Rovers (tenth) qualified for the Intertoto Cup as the highest-placed team who applied for the competition but who failed to earn an automatic UEFA Cup spot, as both Reading (eighth) and Portsmouth (ninth) did not apply. Aston Villa nearly gained a place in the UEFA Cup via the European Fair Play League draw. Their name was placed in the hat by virtue of Spurs, the 2006–07 FA Premier League Fair Play winners, already having qualified for the competition, but Villa missed out, losing to the representatives from Finland and Norway.

## ❧ CHELSEA'S UNLUCKY DOZEN ❧

Chelsea endured a torrid sequence of 12 successive Premiership games without a win in the 1992–93 season, the worst run of winless games of any of the 22 teams that season.

## ✄ FINAL PREMIERSHIP TABLE 2004–2005 ✄

| Pos | Team | P | W | D | L | F | A | Pts |
|-----|------|---|---|---|---|---|---|-----|
| 1. | Chelsea (C) | 38 | 29 | 8 | 1 | 72 | 15 | 95 |
| 2. | Arsenal | 38 | 25 | 8 | 5 | 87 | 36 | 83 |
| 3. | Manchester United | 38 | 22 | 11 | 5 | 57 | 26 | 77 |
| 4. | Everton | 38 | 18 | 7 | 13 | 45 | 46 | 61 |
| 5. | Liverpool | 38 | 17 | 7 | 14 | 52 | 41 | 58 |
| 6. | Bolton Wanderers | 38 | 16 | 10 | 12 | 49 | 44 | 58 |
| 7. | Middlesbrough | 38 | 14 | 13 | 11 | 53 | 46 | 55 |
| 8. | Manchester City | 38 | 13 | 13 | 12 | 47 | 39 | 52 |
| 9. | Tottenham Hotspur | 38 | 14 | 10 | 14 | 47 | 41 | 52 |
| 10. | Aston Villa | 38 | 12 | 11 | 15 | 45 | 52 | 47 |
| 11. | Charlton Athletic | 38 | 12 | 10 | 16 | 42 | 58 | 46 |
| 12. | Birmingham City | 38 | 11 | 12 | 15 | 40 | 46 | 45 |
| 13. | Fulham | 38 | 12 | 8 | 18 | 52 | 60 | 44 |
| 14. | Newcastle United | 38 | 10 | 14 | 14 | 47 | 57 | 44 |
| 15. | Blackburn Rovers | 38 | 9 | 15 | 14 | 32 | 43 | 42 |
| 16. | Portsmouth | 38 | 10 | 9 | 19 | 43 | 59 | 39 |
| 17. | West Bromwich Albion | 38 | 6 | 16 | 16 | 36 | 61 | 34 |
| 18. | Crystal Palace (R) | 38 | 7 | 12 | 19 | 41 | 62 | 33 |
| 19. | Norwich City (R) | 38 | 7 | 12 | 19 | 42 | 77 | 33 |
| 20. | Southampton (R) | 38 | 6 | 14 | 18 | 45 | 66 | 32 |

## ✄ BREACH OF CONTRACT SACKING ✄

On 16 March 2001, Tottenham Hotspur sacked manager George Graham for what the club claimed was a breach of contract. Two weeks later, Spurs' former golden boy, Glenn Hoddle, returned to White Hart Lane from Southampton as their new manager and made another former Spurs favourite, Teddy Sheringham, his first purchase. However, Hoddle's departure from the Saints went down badly with the club's fans.

## ✄ BANK BUSTERS ✄

In late January 1995, Manchester United set a new British transfer record when they signed Andy Cole from Newcastle United for £7 million (£6 million plus the £1m-rated Keith Gillespie).

## ✄ TIGANA WALKS ✄

In March 2003 Jean Tigana left his position as manager of Fulham and was succeeded by club captain Chris Coleman.

## THE TINKER MAN TAKES CHARGE

In September 2000, Chelsea sacked their Italian manager Gianluca Vialli and replaced him with another Italian, Claudio Ranieri. During his time in charge at Stamford Bridge Ranieri was dubbed the "Tinker Man" by the British press on account of the number of times he changed his starting line-up.

## FROM WELSH DRAGON TO ROVER

In September 2004, Mark Hughes handed in his resignation as the manager of the Welsh national side to take up his new appointment as the manager of Blackburn Rovers. Hughes, nicknamed "Sparky", succeeded Graeme Souness, who became manager of Newcastle United.

## POWER SWITCH IN LONDON

When Chelsea retained the Premier League title in the 2005–06 season, Arsenal, who had the Premiership crown three times, were a distant 24 points behind their London rivals in fourth place. It was the first time Arsene Wenger's team had finished outside the top three since he took charge of the Gunners in 1996.

## A REAL DOG-FIGHT

In each of the last three weekends of the 2004–05 Premier League season the team that was sitting bottom of the Premiership table at the start of the weekend finished it outside the drop zone.

## OVER THE HALF

Manchester United's David Beckham scored a goal from his own half against Wimbledon at Selhurst Park on the opening day of the 1996–97 season. His speculative shot sailed 55 yards and over the head of the Dons' keeper Neil Sullivan.

## EAGLES SWOOP INTO DIVISION ONE

Crystal Palace ended season 1992–93 with 49 points from 42 Premiership games and were relegated on goal difference. Their points tally equalled the highest of any club ever to be relegated from the top flight of English football.

# ⚽ 2007–08 PREMIER LEAGUE CLUB MASCOTS ⚽

⚜ Beau Brummie (dog) – Birmingham City ⚜
⚜ Billy the Badger/Terry Bytes – Fulham ⚜
⚜ Bubbles the Bear/Herbie the Hammer – West Ham United ⚜
⚜ Chirpy Cockerel – Tottenham Hotspur ⚜
⚜ Fred the Red – Manchester United ⚜
⚜ Frogmore the Frog – Portsmouth ⚜
⚜ Gunnersaurus Rex – Arsenal ⚜
⚜ Hercules the Lion – Aston Villa ⚜
⚜ JJ and B – Wigan Athletic ⚜
⚜ Kingsley Royal (lion) – Reading ⚜
⚜ Lofty the Lion – Bolton Wanderers ⚜
⚜ Monty Magpie – Newcastle United ⚜
⚜ Moonchester (space alien) – Manchester City ⚜
⚜ Mr Toffee – Everton ⚜
⚜ Rammie – Derby County ⚜
⚜ Roar Lion – Blackburn Rovers ⚜
⚜ Roary the Lion – Middlesbrough ⚜
⚜ Samson and Delilah (black cats) – Sunderland ⚜
⚜ Stamford Lion – Chelsea ⚜

***Did You Know That?***
Liverpool don't have a mascot.

## ⚽ AN AMAZING TURNAROUND ⚽

Micky Adams, who played for Southampton in the Premiership during the 1993–94 season, guided Fulham into Division Two at the end of the 1996–97 season. Amazingly, just 18 months earlier, the London club lay in 23$^{rd}$ place in Division Three, 91$^{st}$ (out of 92 league clubs) in the whole Football League.

## ⚽ A HAT-TRICK OF HAMMERINGS ⚽

Over the space of nine days in March 2008, West Ham United suffered three consecutive 4–0 defeats in the Premier League. The tale of misery went as follows:

| Date | Opponents | Venue |
|------|-----------|-------|
| 1 March | Chelsea | Upton Park |
| 5 March | Liverpool | Anfield |
| 9 March | Tottenham Hotspur | White Hart Lane |

## ❧ FULL HOUSE AT THE THEATRE OF DREAMS ❧

Manchester United's 4–1 hammering of Lancashire rivals Blackburn Rovers at Old Trafford en route to winning the 2007 Premier League title was attended by a crowd of 76,098. The bumper crowd is United's all-time record home attendance and it is also the highest-ever attendance for a Premiership game. Of the 20 clubs in the Premier League in the 2007–08 season only Manchester United has set their record home attendance in a Premier League game.

## ❧ NOT A VERY WISE MOVE ❧

During the 1994–95 season Chelsea's Dennis Wise was involved in a late-night scuffle with a taxi driver in London and was subsequently convicted of criminal damage and assault. The court sentenced Wise to three months in prison, but the conviction and prison sentence were overturned on appeal.

## ❧ THIRD TIME LUCKY ❧

After two successive Wembley defeats for Leicester City in the Division One play-off final, Brian Little finally guided them into the FA Premier League for season 1994–95 when the Foxes beat Derby 2–1 the play-off final. They were joined in the top flight by Crystal Palace, First Division champions in 1993–94, and runners-up Nottingham Forest.

## ❧ A ROYAL SEASON ❧

The 2006–07 season saw Reading playing in the top flight for the first time in their 135-year history. The Royals got off to a good start too, winning their inaugural Premiership game against Middlesbrough 3–2.

## ❧ THE INCREDIBLE SULK ❧

Nicolas Anelka ended the 1998–99 season as the Premier League's joint top goalscorer, on 18 goals, with Leeds United's Jimmy Floyd Hasselbaink, Liverpool's Michael Owen and Manchester United's Dwight Yorke. He was also named the PFA Young Player of the Year. However, it was his final season with the Gunners, as he joined Real Madrid for £22.2 million. Anelka has been known as a loner throughout his career, and because of the difficulty he had in getting on with team-mates, he was nicknamed "The Incredible Sulk".

## ❧ PREMIERSHIP TALK (21) ❧

"It's getting tickly now – squeaky-bum time, I call it."
*Sir Alex Ferguson on the 2002–03 end-of-season title race won by United*

## ❧ EVERTON TIGERS ❧

In season 2007–08 Everton FC entered a team in the British Basketball League, the Everton Tigers.

## ❧ BORO LAND MACCARONE ❧

Prior to the start of the 2002–03 season Middlesbrough broke the club record transfer fee by paying £8.15 million for the services of the Italian international striker Massimo Maccarone from Empoli. The 21-year-old had made the front pages of the Italain newspapers in March 2002 when he became the first Serie B player to be selected for the Italian national side in 20 years. In his first season at The Riverside he scored nine times, but he never really settled in Middlesbrough. During season 2004–05 he was loaned out to Parma in Serie A before returning to Boro for the start of the 2005–06 Premiership campaign. He joined the Italian club Siena in early 2007 on a free transfer.

## ❧ TROPHYLESS GUNNERS ❧

On 12 May 2001 Arsenal faced Liverpool in the FA Cup final, the first to be played at the Millennium Stadium, Cardiff, while Wembley Stadium was being rebuilt. The Gunners took the lead in the game and looked likely to end the season with their first piece of silverware in three seasons only to see Michael Owen score two goals in the last five minutes and hand the FA Cup to the Anfield club. Going into the game Arsenal had just finished runners-up to Manchester United in the Premier League for the third season on the trot.

## ❧ MAGPIES SEEING DOUBLE ❧

Newcastle United ended the 1996–97 season in exactly the same spot where they ended the previous season, runners-up to Manchester United. However, this time the Geordies trailed seven points behind United, three more than had been the case the last campaign.

## ❧ TRACTOR BOYS MOWED DOWN ❧

The 1994–95 season was one of the worst in Ipswich Town's history. The Tractor Boys conceded 92 Premiership goals and managed a meagre seven wins all season (in 42 league games plus the League Cup and FA Cup). Their 29 Premiership defeats including a humiliating 9–0 loss at Manchester United.

## ❧ A UNIQUE DOUBLE ❧

Mark Walters was the first player to score for Liverpool in the Premier League, on 19 August 1992 against Sheffield United at Anfield, and also the first to score a hat-trick for Liverpool in the Premier League, on 17 April 1993 against Coventry City at Anfield.

## ❧ AN OLD VILLAN RETURNS TO THE PARK ❧

On 24 January 2002, John Gregory resigned as manager of Aston Villa after four years in charge. He was replaced by the former England manager Graham Taylor, who had previously guided Aston Villa into the First Division in 1987–88 and to a championship runners-up spot in 1989–90. This success with Aston Villa, plus his earlier work at Watford, prompted the Football Association to come looking for Taylor's services, and he was appointed England manager after Bobby Robson stepped down from the role following the 1990 World Cup finals. Villa ended 2001–02 eighth in the Premiership table – their tenth consecutive top-ten finish.

## ❧ UNITED GIVE ROVERS EUROPEAN BERTH ❧

Manchester United's second-place finish behind Chelsea in the 2005–06 Premier League (guaranteeing them UEFA Champions League football in 2006–07) added to their League Cup success (a 4–0 win over Premiership new boys Wigan Athletic at the Millennium Stadium, Cardiff) meant that the Red Devils' place in the UEFA Cup went to the team that finished sixth in the Premier League table, Blackburn Rovers.

## ❧ LEAKY LEEDS GOAL DROUGHT ❧

In 1996–97 George Graham's Leeds United scored fewer goals than any other Premier League side (28) yet still managed to end the season in a secure 11th position. They conceded 38 goals.

## ℜ ALAN SHEARER, OBE ℜ

Alan Shearer was born in Newcastle-upon-Tyne on 13 August 1970. At the age of 16, while playing as a schoolboy at the famous Wallsend Boys Club, the young striker was rejected by Newcastle United and instead signed as an apprentice for Southampton. On 26 March 1988 he made his first-team debut as a substitute against Chelsea and, a fortnight later, in his first start, scored a hat-trick against Arsenal. At 17 years and 8 months, he became the youngest player ever to score a hat-trick in top-flight English football, breaking Jimmy Greaves' 30-year-old record.

On 19 February 1992, Shearer won his first full England cap and he scored on his international debut against France at Wembley in a 2–0 win. He was a member of the England squad that qualified for that year's European Championships in Sweden, making one appearance at the finals. Alan was, however, the obvious replacement for the retiring Gary Lineker. In 1992 he left the Saints and signed for Blackburn Rovers for a £3.6 million transfer fee, a British record. It was at Ewood Park that he won his only major club honour in the game, the FA Premier League title in season 1994–95. He was voted the PFA Player of the Year for 1994–95 and received the same award from his peers two years later.

At the 1996 European Championships, Alan won the competition's Golden Boot award with five goals. Later in the summer of 1996, Newcastle paid a world record £15 million to Blackburn Rovers to secure his services. Alan helped England to qualify for the 1998 World Cup finals and, in 1999, Kevin Keegan made him captain. Shearer was an ever-present as England reached the 2000 European Championships. In the finals Alan headed the winner against Germany, but England were knocked out at the group stage, following a 3–2 loss to Romania in Charleroi. He scored his 30th and final England goal that night, in his 63rd appearance, but he retired from international football following the competition.

On 18 January 2003, Alan scored a goal after only ten seconds for Newcastle United against Manchester City, equalling the record for the fastest goal ever scored in the FA Premier League and also that for the fastest goal ever scored by a Newcastle player, matching Jackie Milburn's strike in November 1947. In January 2006, he scored his 200th goal for Newcastle to break Milburn's record for the club. Alan retired at the end of the 2005–06 season, having notched up 206 goals for the Magpies and a Premier League record of 261. A part-time pundit in his playing days, Alan is now regular football analyst on television.

### *Did You Know That?*
Alan had a cameo role in the 2005 movie, *Goal!*

## ❧ BACK UP WHERE THEY BELONG ❧

Manchester United's 4–0 win over Wigan Athletic at Old Trafford on 6 October 2007 sent the Red Devils to the top of the Premiership table for the first time since they won the Premiership crown at the end of the 2006–07 season.

## ❧ AL THE FOURTEENTH ❧

When Alan Shearer was signed from Blackburn Rovers for a world-record transfer fee of £15 million in July 1996, he was Kevin Keegan's 14th and last eight-figure purchase for the club during his first spell in charge of the Magpies (1992–97).

## ❧ DOPEY STRIKER ❧

In February 1995, Crystal Palace striker Chris Armstrong failed a random drugs test, having tested positive for cannabis. Armstrong had no hesitation in openly admitting he had done wrong and agreed to undergo a rehabilitation programme.

## ❧ REBROV DOWN THE LANE ❧

When Tottenham Hotspur finished the 1999–2000 season in a disappointing tenth place, they decided to bolster their attack for the 2000–01 season and shelled out a club record £11 million for FC Dynamo Kiev's Ukrainian international striker Sergi Rebrov. Rebrov had just ended the 1999–2000 season as the joint top scorer in the UEFA Champions League with ten goals. Following the sacking of George Graham as Spurs manager in March 2001 Rebrov failed to earn a regular starting place in the team under new boss Glenn Hoddle and over the next few seasons went out on two consecutive loan spells with Turkish club Fenerbahce, before signing a one-year contract with West Ham United in 2004. During his time at Kiev he won the Ukrainian Premier League nine times, the Ukrainian Cup seven times and the Ukrainian Super Cup and, in 2003–04, he won the Turkish league championship with Fenerbahce.

## ❧ CRAZY GANG ON THE MOVE ❧

On 21 June 2004, former Premiership club Wimbledon announced that they would be moving away from South London to Milton Keynes and changing their name to the Milton Keynes Dons.

# ❧ FINAL PREMIERSHIP TABLE 2005–2006 ❧

| Pos Team | P | W | D | L | F | A | Pts |
|---|---|---|---|---|---|---|---|
| 1. Chelsea (C) | 38 | 29 | 4 | 5 | 72 | 22 | 91 |
| 2. Manchester United | 38 | 25 | 8 | 5 | 72 | 34 | 83 |
| 3. Liverpool | 38 | 25 | 7 | 6 | 57 | 25 | 82 |
| 4. Arsenal | 38 | 20 | 7 | 11 | 68 | 31 | 67 |
| 5. Tottenham Hotspur | 38 | 18 | 11 | 9 | 53 | 38 | 65 |
| 6. Blackburn Rovers | 38 | 19 | 6 | 13 | 51 | 42 | 63 |
| 7. Newcastle United | 38 | 17 | 7 | 14 | 47 | 42 | 58 |
| 8. Bolton Wanderers | 38 | 15 | 11 | 12 | 49 | 41 | 56 |
| 9. West Ham United | 38 | 16 | 7 | 15 | 52 | 55 | 55 |
| 10. Wigan Athletic | 38 | 15 | 6 | 17 | 45 | 52 | 51 |
| 11. Everton | 38 | 14 | 8 | 16 | 34 | 49 | 50 |
| 12. Fulham | 38 | 14 | 6 | 18 | 48 | 58 | 48 |
| 13. Charlton Athletic | 38 | 13 | 8 | 17 | 41 | 55 | 47 |
| 14. Middlesbrough | 38 | 12 | 9 | 17 | 48 | 58 | 45 |
| 15. Manchester City | 38 | 13 | 4 | 21 | 43 | 48 | 43 |
| 16. Aston Villa | 38 | 10 | 12 | 16 | 42 | 55 | 42 |
| 17. Portsmouth | 38 | 10 | 8 | 20 | 37 | 62 | 38 |
| 18. Birmingham City (R) | 38 | 8 | 10 | 20 | 28 | 50 | 34 |
| 19. West Bromwich Albion (R) | 38 | 7 | 9 | 22 | 31 | 58 | 30 |
| 20. Sunderland (R) | 38 | 3 | 6 | 29 | 26 | 69 | 15 |

## ❧ LITTLE BIG MEN ❧

The following table lists the seven smallest players playing in the Premier League during the 2007–08 season:

| | | |
|---|---|---|
| 1. Aaron Lennon | Tottenham Hotspur | 165cm |
| 2. Shaun Wright-Phillips | Chelsea | 166cm |
| 3. Ross Wallace | Sunderland | 167cm |
| =4. Steed Malbranque | Tottenham Hotspur | 168cm |
| =4. Paul Scholes | Manchester United | 168cm |
| =4. James Sinclair | Bolton Wanderers | 168cm |
| =4. Carlos Tevez | Manchester United | 168cm |

## ❧ FOUR GAMES AND OUT ❧

Peter Reid was sacked by Manchester City after just four games of the 1993–94 Premiership campaign, and Oxford United manager Brian Horton became the new boss at Maine Road. The Citizens had lost their opening four fixtures.

## ॡ PREMIERSHIP TALK (22) ॡ

"They say he's an intelligent man, right? Speaks five languages! I've got a 15-year-old boy from the Ivory Coast who speaks five languages!"
*Sir Alex Ferguson on his nemesis Arsene Wenger*

## ॡ CHASING LIVERPOOL ॡ

Manchester United won their tenth FA Premier League title in the 2007–08 season to make it 17 top-flight championship titles, second only to Liverpool's record of 18 titles.

## ॡ BARCLAYCARD ANYONE? ॡ

The Premiership's tenth season in 2001–02 attracted a new sponsor and became known as the Barclaycard Premier League.

## ॡ CRESTFALLEN CHAMPIONS ॡ

In late October 1996 Blackburn Rovers, Premiership Champions 18 months previously, found themselves bottom of the Premier League table. Following the resignation of manager Ray Harford, Tony Parkes took charge until the end of the season and helped Rovers avoid the drop with a 13th-place finish.

## ॡ BOXING DAY SPOILER ॡ

On Boxing Day 2002, Darren Ambrose scored in the last minute for Ipswich Town in their Premiership encounter with Leicester City. A year later, on Boxing Day 2003, Ambrose was the scourge of Leicester City once again, this time hitting a last-minute winner against them for Newcastle United.

## ॡ SUPER RONNY ॡ

The 2006–07 PFA Players' Player of the Year Award was won by Manchester United's Cristiano Ronaldo. The Portuguese star also scooped the PFA Young Player of the Year Award, making him the first player to win both prestigious awards since Everton's Andy Gray in 1977, who was the only player to have done it before. By picking up the Young Player Award Ronaldo prevented his United team-mate Wayne Rooney from collecting it for a third consecutive year.

# ⁂ INVESTORS FROM ABROAD ⁂

⁘ Randy Lerner (Aston Villa) ⁘
⁘ Mohammed Al Fayed (Fulham) ⁘
⁘ Roman Abramovich (Chelsea) ⁘
⁘ Malcolm Glazer (Manchester United) ⁘
⁘ Alexandre Gaydamak (Portsmouth) ⁘
⁘ Eggert Magnusson (West Ham) ⁘
⁘ Tom Hicks & George Gillett (Liverpool) ⁘
⁘ Thaksin Shinawatra (Manchester City) ⁘

*Did You Know That?*
Roman Abramovich is governor of the province of Chukotka, Russia.

# ⁂ LONG EXILES ⁂

At the end of the 1998–99 season none of the three sides relegated from the Premiership the previous season regained their top-division status. However, Sunderland returned to the Premiership after a two-year exile by virtue of winning the First Division championship and were joined in the top flight by Bradford City and play-off winners Watford. Watford had endured an 11-year exile from the top flight, whereas Bradford City's exile had lasted 11 times longer, 77 years.

# ⁂ A RUUD APPOINTMENT ⁂

When Glenn Hoddle decided to vacate his position as Chelsea manager at the end of the 1995–96 season and take-up his new post as England manager, the Blues acted swiftly and appointed their 33-year-old Dutch superstar Ruud Gullit as player-manager. The Dutch maestro immediately went for the Stamford Bridge chequebook and forked out a club record £4.9 million for the Italian midfielder Roberto Di Matteo.

# ⁂ FOUR SAFE HANDS ⁂

In season 2002–03, Chelsea goalkeeper Carlo Cudicini won the inaugural Barclaycard Golden Gloves Award after keeping 12 clean sheets (the most by any goalkeeper during the season) and only conceding 35 goals. However, the No.1 shirt in the inaugural 2002–03 PFA Team of the Year went to Blackburn Rovers goalkeeper Brad Friedel.

## ♞ FOOTBALL SEARCHING FOR LOST SOUL ♘

In an interview with the *Daily Telegraph* on 6 October 2007, Sunderland manager Roy Keane spoke very frankly about the state of football: "Football has lost its soul and it's definitely for the worse. It is not the game I knew ten years ago. It's changing and it's sad. There are lots of things like kick-off times, small things that make a difference. Clubs are being sold and fans are complaining about prices. I know [Manchester] United fans were complaining last week about having to buy tickets for the Coventry match. Every club is changing, and not always for the good. The day I left the club I had been involved with for a long, long time [United], it was different to the one I joined. That's why I don't really miss playing. United against Arsenal – if you could go back for one game, it would be that. If I was playing Arsenal on the Saturday, my preparation would start on the previous Sunday. Psychologically, you would prepare."

## ♞ THE ACADEMY ♘

In 2000 Liverpool took the decision to fund and build a multimillion-pound football academy in order to continue nurturing and developing their own young talent. This world-class facility, situated at Kirkby and under the expert guidance of academy director and Liverpool legend Steve Heighway, is designed to give every young boy on the club's books the best possible chance of emulating past products of the Liverpool youth system, such as Robbie Fowler, Steve McManaman, Jamie Carragher, Michael Owen and Steven Gerrard.

## ♞ SPURS DENY UNITED THE QUADRUPLE ♘

Manchester United were knocked out of the 1998–99 League Cup by the eventual winners Tottenham Hotspur. It proved to be the only competition United failed to win that season. Otherwise they swept all before them, winning the Premier League, FA Cup and UEFA Champions League.

## ♞ A RETURN TO WINNING WAYS ♘

In 1997–98, his second season in charge of Leeds United, George Graham guided Leeds United, helped by 16 Premiership goals from Jimmy Floyd Hasselbaink, to an eventual fifth place in the Premiership and guaranteed UEFA Cup football for the following season.

## ❦ PREMIERSHIP TALK (23) ❦

"If he was an inch taller he'd be the best centre-half in Britain. His father is six foot two — I'd check the milkman."
*Sir Alex Ferguson on Gary Neville*

## ❦ A MUTUAL PARTING ❦

On 17 October 2007, Bolton Wanderers announced that the club had parted company with manager Sammy Lee by "mutual consent". Lee had only been in the post for six months having taken over the helm from Sam Allardyce in April 2007 after Big Sam moved to Newcastle United. However, things had not gone well for Lee at the Reebok Stadium, and at the time of his departure the club was lying second from bottom of the Premiership, with only one league win in the season so far. It was widely believed that Lee's departure may have been hastened by his falling-out with Gary Speed the previous week.

## ❦ PREMATURE PAY OUT ❦

During the 1997–98 season Manchester United looked on course for a fifth Premiership title as they led the league by 11 points going into March. One turf accountant even paid out on bets placed for United to win the title. However, Arsenal put in a fine run of late season form, including a 1–0 win over United at Old Trafford on 14 March 1998 (cutting United's lead to six points with three games in hand), and pipped United for the crown by a single point.

## ❦ SUPER TED ❦

Teddy Sheringham scored 14 times for Spurs in the Premiership during the 1993–94 season even though restricted by injury to making only 19 appearances for the London club.

## ❦ THE SAINTLY SINNER ❦

When Glenn Hoddle resigned as Southampton manager in late March 2001 to take over at Tottenham Hotspur, the Saints turned to Stuart Gray, whose temporary appointment was made permanent thanks to the club's good run of form under his stewardship. Southampton finished the 2000–01 season in 10th place in the Premier League, a satisfying two places above Hoddle's Spurs.

# ♜ DUTCH PREMIER LEAGUE FANTASY XI ♞

**1**
Edwin
*Van der SAR*
*(MANCHESTER UTD)*

**2**
Giovanni
*Van BRONCKHORST*
*(ARSENAL)*

**5**
Mario
*MELCHIOT*
*(ASTON VILLA)*

**6**
Jaap
*STAM*
*(MANCHESTER UTD)*

**3**
Wilfred
*BOUMA*
*(ASTON VILLA)*

**4**
Ruud
*GULLIT*
*(CHELSEA, CAPT)*

**7**
Edgar
*DAVIDS*
*(TOTTENHAM HOTSPUR)*

**8**
Robin
*Van PERSIE*
*(ARSENAL)*

**9**
Ruud
*Van NISTELROOY*
*(MANCHESTER UTD)*

**10**
Dennis
*BERGKAMP*
*(ARSENAL)*

**11**
Marc
*OVERMARS*
*(ARSENAL)*

*Substitutes*
Ed de GOEIJ *(Chelsea)* • Andre OOIJER *(Blackburn Rovers)*
Denny LANDZAAT *(Wigan Athletic)* • Dirk KUYT *(Liverpool)*
Arjen ROBBEN *(Chelsea)*
*Manager*
Martin JOL *(Tottenham Hotspur)*

***Did You Know That?***
Martin Jol was capped three times by the Netherlands.

## ♜ UNLUCKY 13 FOR REDS IN 200TH DERBY ♞

The Merseyside derby has been the most frequently played derby match in English football history. The 200th Merseyside derby was played at Goodison Park on 11 December 2004 in front of 40,552 fans. It was the 99th meeting at Goodison and the 25th time the two sides had met in the Premier League. But Liverpool's 13th away Premiership derby against Everton proved unlucky as the Toffees won the game 1–0 with a Lee Carsley goal in the 68th minute.

## ♜ LACK-LUSTRE VILLANS ♞

Aston Villa finished the 2002–03 season 16th in the Premiership, just two places and three points clear of relegation. Villa only managed 12 league wins during the campaign, 11 of them coming at Villa Park.

## ❧ WHEN THE RED MIST DESCENDS ❧

When Alan Smith was sent off in Newcastle United's 6–0 capitulation to Manchester United on 12 January 2008 at Old Trafford, it was the seventh time the fiery forward had been sent off in a Premiership game in his career. However, two others have seen the red mist more times than "Smudger":

| Pos | Player | Team(s) | Red Cards |
|---|---|---|---|
| 1. | Duncan Ferguson | Everton, Newcastle United | 8 |
| 1. | Patrick Vieira | Arsenal | 8 |
| 3. | Vinnie Jones | Wimbledon, Chelsea, QPR | 7 |
| 3 | Roy Keane | Nottingham Forest, Man United | 7 |
| 3. | Alan Smith | Leeds Utd, Man Utd, Newcastle Utd | 7 |

## ❧ A MYSTERIOUS DEPARTURE ❧

On 9 May 2001, Harry Redknapp stepped down as manager of West Ham United after seven years in charge. His sudden departure from the Upton Park club, which had finished 15th in the Premiership table, was totally unexpected and remained a mystery. The Hammers appointed first-team coach Glenn Roeder as Redknapp's successor.

## ❧ LATICS HAND TITLE TO UNITED ❧

When Oldham Athletic produced a shock 1–0 win over Aston Villa at Villa Park towards the end of the 1992–93 season, the inaugural Premier League title went to Manchester United.

## ❧ OCEANIA FOOTBALLER OF THE YEAR ❧

The Oceania Footballer of the Year Award is chosen by a forum of southern-hemisphere journalists and is presented to the best footballer from the Oceania region. Australian Harry Kewell, of Liverpool, won it in 2003, having also won it in 1999 when he was at Leeds United. Kewell is the only Liverpool player to have won the award.

## ❧ NO TURKISH DELIGHT IN EUROPE ❧

During the 1996–97 season, Manchester United lost their 40-year unbeaten home record in Europe. The first team to beat United at Old Trafford was Fenerbahce of Turkey, who won a UEFA Champions League Group C match 1–0. United still reached the quarter-finals.

## ALL CHANGE AMONG THE OWLS

Sheffield Wednesday sacked manager Danny Wilson in March 2000 and replaced him with his assistant Peter Shreeves. Shreeves took charge of the Owls until the end of the season, but could not save them from relegation. At the end of the season Paul Jewell (who, ironically, had helped Bradford City avoid the drop from the Premiership in 1999–2000) walked out of Valley Parade to take charge of the Hillsborough club, with Shreeves reverting to his assistant's position. Meanwhile, Bradford City appointed Jewell's assistant, Chris Hutchings, as their new manager.

## ROCKET MEN GO DOWN

Watford set an unwanted Premier League record in 1999–2000. They finished bottom of the table with just 24 points, the lowest number in Premiership history (a record subsequently broken on two occasions, most recently by 11-point Derby County in 2007–08). Of the three clubs promoted to the Premiership at the start of the season, Watford was the only one to be relegated – both Bradford City and Sunderland survived at the expense of Sheffield Wednesday and Wimbledon.

## ALL WRIGHT

Ian Wright is the only player to have been the Golden Boot winner (top goalscorer) in both the old First Division and the Premier League. He headed the list with 29 goals in 1991–92, the last season of the old First Division, and in the Premier League with 24 goals in 1996–97.

## FOXES NO LONGER IN THE HUNT

At the end of September 2001, Leicester City sacked manager Peter Taylor and replaced him with Dave Bassett following a disappointing start to the season. Mickey Adams was brought in as Bassett's assistant. However, the Foxes were unable to stop the slide into Division One and were relegated after losing 1–0 at home to Manchester United on 6 April 2002. Leicester City finished bottom of the Premiership table with just 28 points from their 38 Premiership games. Prior to their relegation, Bassett moved upstairs at Filbert Street to become the club's director of football, and Adams was promoted to the manager's seat, with former Cardiff City manager Alan Cork being named as Adams' assistant.

## ॐ FINAL PREMIERSHIP TABLE 2006–2007 ॐ

| Pos Team | P | W | D | L | F | A | Pts |
|---|---|---|---|---|---|---|---|
| 1. Manchester United (C) | 38 | 28 | 5 | 5 | 83 | 27 | 89 |
| 2. Chelsea | 38 | 24 | 11 | 3 | 64 | 24 | 83 |
| 3. Liverpool | 38 | 20 | 8 | 10 | 57 | 27 | 68 |
| 4. Arsenal | 38 | 19 | 11 | 8 | 63 | 35 | 68 |
| 5. Tottenham Hotspur | 38 | 17 | 9 | 12 | 57 | 54 | 60 |
| 6. Everton | 38 | 15 | 13 | 10 | 52 | 36 | 58 |
| 7. Bolton Wanderers | 38 | 16 | 8 | 14 | 47 | 52 | 56 |
| 8. Reading | 38 | 16 | 7 | 15 | 52 | 47 | 55 |
| 9. Portsmouth | 38 | 14 | 12 | 12 | 45 | 42 | 54 |
| 10. Blackburn Rovers | 38 | 15 | 7 | 16 | 52 | 54 | 52 |
| 11. Aston Villa | 38 | 11 | 17 | 10 | 43 | 41 | 50 |
| 12. Middlesbrough | 38 | 12 | 10 | 16 | 44 | 49 | 46 |
| 13. Newcastle United | 38 | 11 | 10 | 17 | 38 | 47 | 43 |
| 14. Manchester City | 38 | 11 | 9 | 18 | 29 | 44 | 42 |
| 15. West Ham United | 38 | 12 | 5 | 21 | 35 | 59 | 41 |
| 16. Fulham | 38 | 8 | 15 | 15 | 38 | 60 | 39 |
| 17. Wigan Athletic | 38 | 10 | 8 | 20 | 37 | 59 | 38 |
| 18. Sheffield United (R) | 38 | 10 | 8 | 20 | 32 | 55 | 38 |
| 19. Charlton Athletic (R) | 38 | 8 | 10 | 20 | 34 | 60 | 34 |
| 20. Watford (R) | 38 | 5 | 13 | 20 | 29 | 59 | 28 |

## ॐ FIFA SCRAP GOAL-LINE TRIALS ॐ

Following a meeting in Zurich, Switzerland, on 14 March 2008, FIFA president Sepp Blatter announced that goal-line technology experiments were being stopped immediately. The reason was that there had been issues of reliability and their suitability for football. This came as a blow to both the the Football Association and the Premier League, who had supported the trials that had only been started earlier in the month. The Premier League and FA had hoped to introduce the "Hawkeye" system – versions of which are used in tennis and cricket – in time for the start of the 2009–10 season.

## ॐ LEADING ALL THE WAY ॐ

On 23 August 1993, Manchester United beat Aston Villa, Premiership runners-up to United in the previous season, 2–1 at Villa Park to move to top place in the Premiership table. Amazingly, United stayed there for the rest of the season and, eight months later, were crowned champions for the second successive year.

# 🎽 SIR TREVOR STEPS INTO THE BREACH 🎽

In April 2003, West Ham manager Glenn Roeder was forced to stand down temporarily when he after being diagnosed with a brain tumour. Former West Ham legend Sir Trevor Brooking took charge until Glenn was fit enough to return. However, not even Brooking could prevent West Ham from being relegated after they finished 18th in the Premiership table that season. Sunderland, who finished bottom and West Bromwich Albion, 19th, also went down with the Hammers.

# 🎽 PREMIERSHIP TALK (24) 🎽

"At a young age winning is not the most important thing... the important thing is to develop creative and skilled players with good confidence."
*Arsenal manager Arsene Wenger*

# 🎽 WE'LL BE BACK 🎽

After they were relegated to Division One at the end of the 1993–94 season, John Gorman the manager of Swindon Town said that the Robins "won't be in Division One for long". Gorman was right: the Robins went on a downward spiral, including relegation to Division Two at the end of the 2005–06 season.

# 🎽 YOUNG MICHAEL OWEN 🎽

Liverpool's 18-year-old striker Michael Owen scored 18 Premier League goals in 36 games in the 1997–98 season, helping Liverpool to third place in the table and UEFA Cup football for season 1998–99. Owen's 18 goals made him the Premiership's joint top goalscorer and won him both the PFA Young Player of the Year Award and the Carling Player of the Year Award, as well as place in Glenn Hoddle's England 1998 World Cup finals squad.

# 🎽 CANARIES FALL OUT OF THE NEST 🎽

Norwich City finished third in the inaugural Premiership table in 1992–93. Two years later they finished 20th and were relegated after spending nine years in the top flight. From the start of the season to the beginning of the following season they had three managers: John Deehan, Gary Megson (player-manager) and Martin O'Neill.

## ✿ PREMIERSHIP TALK (19) ✿

"He was certainly full of it, calling me 'Boss' and 'Big Man' when we had our post-match drink after the first leg. But it would help if his greetings were accompanied by a decent glass of wine. What he gave me was paint-stripper."
*Sir Alex Ferguson on Jose Mourinho*

## ✿ THE £100M MAN ✿

In his four years in charge of Leeds United (1998–99 to 2001–02) David O'Leary spent £100 million in the transfer market, but failed to bring any silverware to Elland Road.

## ✿ OCTUPUS TURNS INTO A MAGPIE ✿

In early 1996 Kevin Keegan brought the Colombian international Faustino Hernan Asprilla Hinestroza to Newcastle United from Parma. Asprilla had two nicknames, "The Octopus" and "Two-Goal Tino", the former on account of his flexible style of play and the latter because he usually scored for his teams in twos.

## ✿ THAT SINKING FEELING ✿

Nottingham Forest suffered their third relegation from the Premier League in seven seasons at the end of the 1998–99 season; they had also gone down in 1992–93 and 1996–97. Forest finished bottom of the table while Blackburn Rovers, Premiership champions in 1994–95, also went down along with Charlton Athletic.

## ✿ THERE'S ONLY TWO KEANOS ✿

During the 1999–2000 season Robbie Keane scored 12 goals in 34 Premier League appearances for Coventry City. Meanwhile the other R. Keane, Roy, captained Manchester United to the Premier League title.

## ✿ THREE FOXES IN THE DOCK ✿

On 5 March 2004, three Leicester City players – Paul Dickov, Keith Gillespie and Frank Sinclair – were charged with sexual assault while the Premiership club was on a training camp in La Manga, Spain. However, all charges against them were dropped in May 2004.

## ※ EAGLES SWOOP BEFORE FALLING ※

In 1995 newly promoted Crystal Palace reached the semi-finals of both the FA Cup and League Cup competitions, but their excellent domestic Cup form did not carry over into their Premiership, as they made an instant return to the First Division. In a strange twist of fate the Eagles finished in the last four of all the competitions they entered in 1994–95, but that season, unfortunately, last four in the Premiership meant relegation.

## ※ THE MAN OF MANY TONGUES ※

Arsene Wenger, the manager of Arsenal, is fluent in French, Alsatian, English and German and also speaks Italian, Japanese and Spanish.

## ※ CUP-LOSERS GET CUP WINNERS' CUP SPOT ※

Manchester United beat Liverpool in the 1996 FA Cup final thanks to a late goal from their French talisman Eric Cantona. The win gave United the Double for the second time in the club's history. Their Premiership success meant that United would play in the Champions League in 1996–97, while Liverpool would take their place in the European Cup Winners' Cup.

## ※ A HISTORIC SEASON ※

The 2001–02 Premiership season was notable for the fact that it was the first time in the competition's history that all three promoted teams avoided relegation – Blackburn Rovers (finished tenth), Fulham (13th) and Bolton Wanderers (16th).

## ※ UNITED'S DOZEN ※

In season 1998–99 Manchester United won their fifth Premier League title in seven years, their 12th Championship success.

## ※ PREMIERSHIP TALK (25) ※

"If you have no eggs, you have no omelette. And it also depends on the quality of the eggs. In the supermarket you have class one eggs, and you also have class two and class three. Some are more expensive than others and they give you better omelettes."
*Former Chelsea manager Jose Mourinho*

# ❧ FRENCH PREMIER LEAGUE FANTASY XI ❧

**1**
Fabien
***BARTHEZ***
*(MANCHESTER UTD)*

**2**
Mikael
***SILVESTRE***
*(MANCHESTER UTD)*

**6**
Laurent
***BLANC***
*(MANCHESTER UTD)*

**5**
William
***GALLAS***
*(CHELSEA & ARSENAL)*

**3**
Patrice
***EVRA***
*(MANCHESTER UTD)*

**7**
Eric
***CANTONA***
*(LEEDS UTD & MANCHESTER UTD capt.)*

**4**
Patrick
***VIEIRA***
*(ARSENAL)*

**8**
Claude
***MAKELELE***
*(CHELSEA)*

**9**
Nicolas
***ANELKA***
*(BOLTON WANDERERS et al)*

**10**
Thierry
***HENRY***
*(ARSENAL)*

**11**
Robert
***PIRES***
*(ARSENAL)*

*Substitutes*
Lionel ***PEREZ*** *(Sunderland)* • Bakary ***SAGNA*** *(Arsenal)*
Mathieu ***FLAMINI*** *(Arsenal)* • David ***GINOLA*** *(Newcastle Utd & Tottenham)*
Louis ***SAHA*** *(Manchester Utd)*
*Manager*
Arsene ***WENGER*** OBE *(Arsenal)*

### *Did You Know That?*
Claude Makelele was born in Kinshasa, Zaire (now the Democratic Republic of the Congo) and Patrice Evra was born in Dakar, Senegal.

## ❧ LIVERPOOL BACK IN EUROPE ❧

Liverpool finished third in the Premiership in season 2000–01, 11 points behind champions Manchester United, and qualified for the 2001–02 UEFA Champions League. Liverpool had not participated in Europe's premier club competition since the fateful 1985 final at Heysel, where 39 Juventus fans were killed. After the 1985 European Cup final, in which Juventus beat Liverpool 1–0, UEFA banned all English clubs from European football for six years.

## ❧ ADDICKS ON THE RISE ❧

Charlton Athletic finished ninth in the Premiership in the 2000–01 season, the Addicks' highest league position since the 1950s.

# ✌ FOLLOWING THE SPECIAL ONE ✌

When Jose Mourinho left Chelsea on 20 September 2007, he was replaced by Chelsea's director of football, Avram Grant, just 74 days after he arrived at Stamford Bridge. Grant had previously coached in Israel, at Maccabi Tel Aviv (1991–95 & 1997–2000) and Maccabi Haifa (2000–02). He led Maccabi Tel Aviv to the Liga Leumit (Israeli championship) in 1992 and 1995 and to Israeli Cup success in 1994 and guided Maccabi Haifa to Liga Leumit titles in 2001 and 2002. In May 2002 he was appointed the national coach of Israel and almost steered them to the 2006 World Cup finals. Despite being unbeaten in their group (W4, D6) they finished third behind France and Switzerland. In June 2006, Portsmouth appointed him as their technical director and on 8 July 2007 Roman Abramovich brought him to Chelsea. "Avram is here to help," said Jose Mourinho, speaking on Chelsea's pre-season 2007 tour of the USA. "He does not want to create problems for people."

## ✌ A BRIEF STAY ✌

Bolton Wanderers (Division One champions in 1996–97), Barnsley (runners-up) and Crystal Palace (play-off final winners) were all promoted to the Premiership for the 1997–98 season. At the end of the season all three newly promoted teams dropped back into Division One.

## ✌ BAD TRAVELLERS ✌

Leeds United, winners of the last-ever Division One championship in 1991–92, failed to win any of their 21 away games during the inaugural FA Premier League season in 1992–93. Their final league position was 17th, three places above a relegation berth. It marked a huge fall from grace.

## ✌ A MAN FOR ALL LEAGUES ✌

Steve Finnan is the only player to have played in the Premier League, League Divisions One, Two and Three, the Football Conference, the League Cup, the FA Cup, the UEFA Cup, the UEFA Champions League and the FIFA World Cup finals. The Irish international achieved this feat with Welling United (1993–95), Birmingham City (1995–96), Notts County (1996–98), Fulham (1998–2003) and Liverpool (2003–08).

## ALL WHITE, ALL WRONG

Following the Premiership games over the weekend of 20–21 October 2007, the three teams lying at the foot of the Premiership table all had white jerseys as their home kit: Tottenham Hotspur (18th), Bolton Wanderers (19th) and Derby County (20th).

## WHEN THREE BECOMES TWO

The 1995–96 season was the first since the Premiership began three years earlier in which only two sides were promoted from the First Division, Middlesbrough as champions and play-off winners Bolton Wanderers.

## IF ONLY

In 1992–93, Blackburn Rovers ended the inaugural Premiership season in fourth place, but they might have finished higher had Alan Shearer not been ruled out of action in December after scoring 16 goals in his first 21 league appearances. His knee injury kept him out of action until the following season.

## A MARK OF RESPECT FOR PRINCESS DI

On 31 August 1997, the Premiership game between Liverpool and Newcastle United was postponed as a mark of respect for Diana, Princess of Wales, who had died early that morning in a car crash in Paris. On 6 September, the day of her funeral, all Premiership and Football League matches were postponed.

## THE GREAT DANE

Peter Schmeichel is the only player to have won the Premier League, FA Cup, League Cup, Charity Shield, UEFA Champions League, UEFA Super Cup (all with Manchester United), Intertoto Cup (with Aston Villa) and the European Championships (with Denmark).

## THE CUP KINGS

In the process of winning the Treble in 1998–99, Manchester United also won their third domestic Double (after those of 1993–94 and 1995–96), while their 2–0 FA Cup final win over Newcastle United at Wembley was a record 10th win for a club in the competition.

## ✂ LEADING PREMIERSHIP GOALSCORERS ✂

These players have scored the most goals in a Premiership season:

| Pos Player | Team | Goals | Season |
|---|---|---|---|
| =1. Andy Cole | Newcastle United | 34 | 1993–94 |
| =1. Alan Shearer | Blackburn Rovers | 34 | 1994–95* |
| =3. Alan Shearer | Blackburn Rovers | 31 | 1993–94 |
| =3. Alan Shearer | Blackburn Rovers | 31 | 1995–96 |
| =3. Cristiano Ronaldo | Manchester United | 31 | 2007–08* |
| =7. Kevin Phillips | Sunderland | 30 | 1999–2000 |
| =7. Thierry Henry | Arsenal | 30 | 2003–04* |
| 8. Robbie Fowler | Liverpool | 28 | 1995–96 |
| 9. Thierry Henry | Arsenal | 27 | 2005–06 |
| =10. Matt Le Tissier | Southampton | 25 | 1993–94 |
| =10. Chris Sutton | Norwich City | 25 | 1993–94 |
| =10. Robbie Fowler | Liverpool | 25 | 1994–95 |
| =10. Les Ferdinand | Newcastle United | 25 | 1995–96 |
| =10. Alan Shearer | Newcastle United | 25 | 1996–97 |
| =10. Ruud van Nistelrooy | Manchester United | 25 | 2002–03* |
| =10. Thierry Henry | Arsenal | 25 | 2004–05 |
| =17. Les Ferdinand | Queen's Park Rangers | 24 | 1994–95 |
| =17. Thierry Henry | Arsenal | 24 | 2001–02* |
| =17. Thierry Henry | Arsenal | 24 | 2002–03 |
| =17. Emmanuel Adebayor | Arsenal | 24 | 2007–08 |
| =17. Fernando Torres | Liverpool | 24 | 2007–08 |

*Premier League champions that season*

## ✂ LIVERPOOL BREAK THE BANK ✂

In the summer of 1995 Liverpool smashed the British transfer record with the £8.4m purchase of Nottingham Forest's Stan Collymore.

## ✂ GUNNERS BEGIN TO FIRE ✂

In 1996–97, in his first full season as the manager of the Gunners, Arsene Wenger took Arsenal to third place in the Premiership.

## ✂ AWAY-DAY REVELLERS ✂

On their way to winning the Double in 2001–02, Arsenal were the only side not to lose a Premiership match away from home during the whole season and to score in all 38 Premiership matches.

# ❧ ARSENE WENGER OBE ❧

Arsene Wenger was born in Strasbourg, France, on 22 October 1949. Compared to his managerial career, however, his playing career was modest. He played as a defender for various amateur clubs while studying at Strasbourg's Robert Schuman University, obtaining a Masters degree in economics. After turning pro in 1978 he played for Strasbourg 12 times, including a UEFA Cup game, before obtaining a manager's diploma and being appointed coach of Strasbourg's youth team.

In 1984, Nancy gave Wenger his first taste of management, but he failed to turn the team's fortunes around and they were relegated to Ligue 2 in 1986–87. He then moved on to Monaco, where he enjoyed immediate success, winning Ligue 1 in 1987–88. In 1990–91 he guided them to French Cup success and was responsible for signing high-profile players for the club, including Glenn Hoddle, Jurgen Klinsmann and George Weah. After turning down advances from Bayern Munich and the French national team, Wenger was sacked by Monaco following a poor start to the 1994–95 season. He took charge of Nagoya Grampus Eight in the Japanese J-League, where he won the Emperor's Cup and Japanese J-League Super Cup in 1996.

Following the resignation of Bruce Rioch as Arsenal manager in August 1996, Wenger agreed to take charge of the London club, becoming their first foreign manager, but only after ensuring that the club signed French midfielders Remi Garde and Patrick Vieira. In only his second season in charge (1997–98), Arsenal won the Double of Premier League and FA Cup and so began a long-standing rivalry with Manchester United, who won titles in 1999, 2000 and 2001, with Arsenal finishing runners-up on all three occasions. Wenger guided the Gunners to their third Double in 2001–02, their second under his charge, and although the following season United regained the Premiership crown (Arsenal, again, were runners-up), Arsenal reclaimed it in 2003–04.

Arsenal won the FA Cup in 2003 and 2005, and also reached the finals of the 2000 UEFA Cup final and 2006 UEFA Champions League final under Wenger. In 2004–05 and 2005–06 both Wenger and Sir Alex Ferguson had to take back seats as Jose Mourinho and Chelsea took the championship. Arsenal finished runners-up in 2004–05, but in the following two seasons their young side had to settle for fourth place. Arsenal often were criticized for their indiscipline early in Wenger's reign, receiving 52 red cards between 1996 and 2003, but they won the Premier League's Fair Play Award in 2004 and 2005.

### Did You Know That?
Wenger is the only non-British manager to win the Double in England.

## ✄ STRACHAN THE SAGE ✄

*Some gems from* **Gordon Strachan**
*Reporter:* "Welcome to Southampton Football Club. Do you think you are the right man to turn things around?"
*Strachan:* "No. I was asked if I thought I was the right man for the job and I said no. I think they should have got George Graham because I'm useless."

*Reporter:* "Gordon, you must be delighted with that result?"
*Strachan:* "You're spot on! You can read me like a book."

*Strachan:* "I've got more important things to think about. I've got a yogurt to finish by today, the expiry date is today. That can be my priority rather than Augustin Delgado."

*Reporter:* "Gordon, can we have a quick word please?"
*Strachan:* "Velocity." [Strachan then walked off.]

*Reporter:* "So, Gordon, in what areas do you think Middlesbrough were better than you today?"
*Strachan:* "What areas? Mainly that big green one out there."

## ✄ A BAD DRIVER ✄

On 22 October 2007, Manchester City's Dietmar Hamann was banned from driving for six months and ordered to pay more than £7,000 in fines for a series of motoring offences. Hamann crashed his Porsche into a fence in Styal, Cheshire, in 2006 and drove away from the scene without reporting the incident to the police.

## ✄ TOP DON ✄

Prior to the start of the 1995–96 season Wimbledon sold Warren Barton to Newcastle United for £4 million, making him the most expensive defender signed by any British club.

## ✄ UNKNOWN TERRITORY FOR UNITED ✄

Manchester United finished third in the 2001–02 Premiership behind champions Arsenal and runners-up Liverpool. It was United's lowest-ever Premiership finish: in the nine years since the league began they had been champions seven times and runners-up twice.

## ❧ FINAL PREMIERSHIP TABLE 2007–2008 ❧

| Pos | Team | P | W | D | L | F | A | Pts |
|---|---|---|---|---|---|---|---|---|
| 1. | Manchester United (C) | 38 | 27 | 6 | 5 | 80 | 22 | 87 |
| 2. | Chelsea | 38 | 25 | 10 | 3 | 65 | 26 | 85 |
| 3. | Arsenal | 38 | 24 | 11 | 3 | 74 | 31 | 83 |
| 4. | Liverpool | 38 | 21 | 13 | 4 | 67 | 28 | 76 |
| 5. | Everton | 38 | 19 | 8 | 11 | 55 | 33 | 65 |
| 6. | Aston Villa | 38 | 16 | 12 | 10 | 71 | 51 | 60 |
| 7. | Blackburn Rovers | 38 | 15 | 13 | 10 | 50 | 48 | 58 |
| 8. | Portsmouth | 38 | 16 | 9 | 13 | 48 | 40 | 57 |
| 9. | Manchester City | 38 | 15 | 10 | 13 | 45 | 53 | 55 |
| 10. | West Ham United | 38 | 13 | 10 | 15 | 42 | 50 | 49 |
| 11. | Tottenham Hotspur | 38 | 11 | 13 | 14 | 66 | 61 | 46 |
| 12. | Newcastle United | 38 | 11 | 10 | 17 | 45 | 65 | 43 |
| 13. | Middlesbrough | 38 | 10 | 12 | 17 | 43 | 54 | 42 |
| 14. | Wigan Athletic | 38 | 10 | 10 | 18 | 34 | 51 | 40 |
| 15. | Sunderland | 38 | 11 | 6 | 21 | 36 | 59 | 39 |
| 16. | Bolton Wanderers | 38 | 9 | 10 | 19 | 36 | 54 | 37 |
| 17. | Fulham | 38 | 8 | 12 | 18 | 38 | 60 | 36 |
| 18. | Reading (R) | 38 | 10 | 6 | 22 | 41 | 66 | 36 |
| 19. | Birmingham City (R) | 38 | 8 | 11 | 19 | 46 | 62 | 35 |
| 20. | Derby County (R) | 38 | 1 | 8 | 29 | 20 | 89 | 11 |

## ❧ MISSING THE BLUES ❧

Birmingham City were the only club in the Premier League in 2007–08 without a single England international in their squad. Arsenal had only one, Theo Walcott.

## ❧ A LOT OF GRASS TO COVER ❧

Aston Villa's home stadium, Villa Park, had the biggest playing area in the Premiership in 2007–08, measuring 115 x 75m. Fratton Park, Portsmouth's home, had the smallest playing area, 100 x 65m.

## ❧ TEVEZ DOES IT AGAIN ❧

Carlos Tevez scored and collected win bonuses in Manchester United's final home game of the season in both 2006–07 and 2007–08. In the first of these, he was playing for West Ham United as they won 1–0 at Old Trafford. Twelve months later, coincidentally also against the Hammers, he was on target for the home team as they won 4–1.

## ❧ GIGGS MATCHES SIR BOBBY ❧

When Ryan Giggs came on as a second-half substitute in Manchester United's 2–0 win over Wigan Athletic at the JJB Stadium on 11 May 2008, he equalled Sir Bobby Charlton's club record of 758 appearances for the club. Sir Bobby was on hand to greet the Welsh Wizard as he left the pitch after the match that clinched his tenth Premier Division champions medal. Giggs also scored the second goal that afternoon, his 101st in the Premiership for his only club.

## ❧ UNAVOIDABLE DROP ❧

On the final day of the 2007–08 season, Reading beat already relegated Derby County 4–0 at Pride Park and Birmingham City saw off Blackburn Rovers 4–1 at St Andrews. Unfortunately for both teams, those victories were not enough to save them from relegation, as Fulham recorded a 1–0 away victory at Portsmouth. Reading had needed to win by seven more goals than Fulham to send the Cottagers down on goal difference.

## ❧ SEEING YELLOW ❧

Chelsea players have been shown more yellow cards than any other club in the history of the Premier League. In the 16 seasons, the following five clubs have seen yellow most often:

| Team | Seasons | Yellow cards | Average |
|---|---|---|---|
| Chelsea | 16 | 932 | 58.25 |
| Everton | 16 | 902 | 56.38 |
| Arsenal | 16 | 871 | 54.44 |
| Tottenham Hotspur | 16 | 831 | 51.94 |
| Blackburn Rovers | 14 | 825 | 59.93 |

## ❧ LONG RANGE AL ❧

Alan Shearer (Blackburn and Newcastle) is the Premier League's record scorer of goals from outside the penalty area. The competition's all-time leading scorer, with 260 goals, netted 35 long-range efforts, two more than David Beckham (Manchester United). Two players are tied for third on the list, Jimmy Floyd Hasselbairtck (Leeds United, Chelsea, Middlesbrough and Charlton), the leading overseas long-range scorer, and Frank Lampard (West Ham and Chelsea) with 30.

# ❧ INDEX ❧